MW01231466

Fourth Down and Long

Feb 2023

Do Right... Right Follows!

Faith, Hope & Love!

Tony Lollar

Fourth Down and Long

◆

Everything Is Possible When You Believe

Tony Lotti

iUniverse, Inc.

New York Lincoln Shanghai

Fourth Down and Long
Everything Is Possible When You Believe

Copyright © 2005 by Tony Lotti

iUniverse books may be ordered through booksellers or by contacting:

iUniverse
2021 Pine Lake Road, Suite 100
Lincoln, NE 68512
www.iuniverse.com
1-800-Authors (1-800-288-4677)

ISBN: 0-595-34285-X (pbk)
ISBN: 0-595-67095-4 (cloth)

Printed in the United States of America

For my family:
You have always been there for me and you are my inspiration.
Thank you.

Contents

Foreword

I heard a quote one day: "Obstacles are things a person sees when he takes his eyes off his goal." I can't remember who said it, but I fell in love with the saying. You see, no matter what your dreams or aspirations are in this world, there will be plenty of obstacles in your path. I set goals for myself early in my life. I knew that nothing came easy, and I learned that lesson while I was still young.

My biggest dream, without a doubt, was to walk into an NFL training camp as a player; if it was the playing field of the New England Patriots, that would be even better. If you know anything about getting into the NFL, well, let's put it this way: probably one in ten million kids gets a chance. How's that for a stretch goal? My other major dream was to be named a collegiate All-American. These were big dreams for a kid who graduated from high school at 5'9" and 170 pounds. Oh yeah, and I ran the forty-yard dash in 5.3 seconds. With that information, my odds shift to one in fifty billion for either the NFL or All-American status, but I'll get to that part later. After achieving those two goals, I had another big one—I wanted to write a book. Those of you who know me well are probably laughing pretty hard right now, but I'll go ahead and fill the rest of you in. I'm far from stupid, but I was just a little lazy when it came to schoolwork. I graduated from high school with about a C+ average, and I earned my bachelor's degree by…well, let's just say I got it! Ever heard the saying that goes: "What do you call the guy who graduated last in his class at medical school?" That's right: *doc-*

tor! I completed and earned the degree; the rest, in my opinion, is immaterial.

I also try very hard not to make excuses for anything; you shouldn't either. You have the power to control your life, and the sooner you take responsibility for your life, the better off you'll be. Everything happens for a reason and is part of God's will. Unfortunately, you have to take the good with the bad. That's life. The main thing to realize is that if you don't like your current situation, then you have to change it. Don't make excuses or blame someone else for it. Set your goals and focus on nothing else. Keep going until you reach them. Don't listen to people who try to drag you down. Misery loves company, and, trust me, unhappy people are recruiting new members all the time. Believe in God and love your family. When things are great and you're on top, "friends" are easy to find. When times are tough, God and your family are all that you have. The good news is that you can always count on those two! I am not naive enough to think that the far-fetched goals I have reached were solely accomplished by me. God and my family played a huge part.

Since I mentioned them, let me go ahead and say that this book is dedicated to both of them. I talk to my Heavenly Father daily and often. We don't always see things the same way, but I know that his plan for me is to love me and shelter me. Eventually, I'll get to ask him why certain things happened. Until then, I'll just keep trusting and believing. All in all, I'm truly blessed. I have the best parents. Even though I unexpectedly lost my dad four years ago, I'm not yet ready to let him go. My family is always there for me. Whether it's a time of celebration or tribulation, I can count on them. My sister, Gina, and my brothers, Mark, Scott, and Vinny, are all younger than me. I've tried to set a good example for all of you, and hopefully, I am an older brother that you can look up to and be proud of. To my wife, Debbie, and my children, Antonia, Anissa, and Anthony: you are the greatest gift and treasure of my life. Nothing on this earth could ever take your place, and I thank God for you all the time. Hopefully, you will be able to keep this book always and know that you were, by far, my greatest accomplishment.

If you only get one thing from this book, get this: *no* dream is too big, and if you're going to dream, then dream *big*. You are your greatest fan and your worst critic. If you want it bad enough and are willing to work for it, you can have it. Don't take yourself too seriously. Laugh once in a while, and sing out loud. Lastly, remember the Golden Rule, and do something nice for someone else.

Good luck,

Tony

1

A Rough Start

I remember when I was a kid, I used to watch college and pro football games with my dad. I was born in Quincy, Massachusetts, but moved to Morrow, Georgia, when I was five years old. My dad worked for Delta Air Lines and was transferred to Atlanta in 1972. Even though our entire family was in Massachusetts, my mom and dad thought we would have a better life in Georgia, and, as usual, they were right. See, when you are a kid, your parents will tell you they are always right. It's not until you become a grown-up with kids of your own that you realize—yeah, they *are* always right.

There is a big difference between growing up in the South and in the North. To our family up North, we were definitely Southerners. To everyone in Georgia, well, we were Italian Yankees. We couldn't win for losing. Because I did grow up in the South, football became my game. Let's face it: there are not a lot of hockey rinks in Georgia. As a matter of fact, there were none.

Because he was from Massachusetts, my dad was a huge New England Patriots fan. He and Grandpa had season tickets, and even after we moved, he remained a die-hard Pats fan. So there you have it: Dad's a Patriots fan; son becomes a Patriots fan. I wanted to give that gift to my dad. I wanted him to have the ability to say that his son was a member of the New England Patriots.

I started playing organized football when I was five, and I fell in love with the sport. I played in the community organization ("rec-ball") every year until I was old enough to play in junior high. My dad coached me in the recreation league one season...and only one season. I never played for a harder coach in my life. It seemed that I had to work twice as hard as the other players so no one could say that I was the starting quarterback because the coach was my dad. I have mixed emotions about recreation ball. Nowadays, the kids just don't seem to have any fun. Unfortunately, I think a lot of dad-coaches try to live out their dreams through their children.

The Early Years - 11 year old YMCA Bulldogs

The Early Years - 12 Year Old Morrow Lake City Chiefs

8th Grade Quarterback - Morrow Jr. High

Things started to get serious for me once I entered high school. Even before I got to high school, my dad would go watch the local high school play football games every Friday night. See, in Georgia, Friday nights in the fall are reserved for high school football. When it came to football, my dad was my motivation. I admit that there were a lot of seasons that I played just for him. He never forced me to play, but it was just that look he had when I was playing. The rule in our house was that you could never quit anything once you started it. If you didn't want to play, that was fine, but once you started, you had to finish. That's a great rule, and now I'm thankful that my parents made it and stuck to it. My parents used to say that once you quit the first time, it gets easier to quit the next time. If there's one thing I'm not, it's a quitter. I am thankful for that lesson, because in life there are many times when you feel like quitting, but you just can't.

After my junior football season in high school, I went to Massachusetts to visit my family and relax. One night, my cousin and I were going out to meet some of his friends and hang out. After we picked up his friends, we went cruising. My cousin, like most kids our age at the time, had an old car that was, let's just say, "nice for the price." I was riding in the backseat on the passenger side, and my brother, Mark, was in the middle. My cousin was driving, and we were just talking about stuff as we rode. What would happen next would be a major setback in my life.

I felt the car start to make a left turn and heard others in the car yell, "Look out!" I looked out my window and saw nothing but headlights. A car coming in the opposite direction slammed into our car, right where I was sitting. I remember the car spinning around after the impact, and that's about all I remember. I was numb on the right side of my body. I had been hit pretty hard before in football, so I thought the numbness would go away.

Then I flew back home to Georgia to see a specialist. The numbness had turned into loss of feeling on my right side, which included my right leg and arm. The official diagnosis was nerve damage to the cervical spine. The impact had stretched the nerves to a point where I lost feeling on that side of my body. The doctors did not know at that time whether the paralysis would be permanent; we would have to wait and see.

I could not attend school, but a teacher was assigned to visit me so I wouldn't have to lose an academic year. My parents set up our living room with a bed and such, so I wouldn't be confined to my bedroom. I would lie there for the next few months wondering if my football days were over. I wasn't concerned about whether or not I would ever walk again or regain the feeling in my right side. I was worried about playing football. I guess that's when I realized that I truly loved to play.

Then, one morning, I woke up and felt pain in my right arm and leg. I have never been so happy to be in pain. It was hurting, but it felt like it does when you hit your funny bone on something. Gradually, the pain started to fade, and the feeling and use of my arm and leg came back. I started rehabilitation exercises, because my focus was on playing football during my senior season.

It was now July 2, 1984. My rehabilitation had gone very well, and I had just got permission from the doctor to play football the day before. The team was having the first workout session of the season, and I was given the go-ahead to participate. It was great to be back around everybody. I was excited, but I had developed a pain in my stomach early that morning. I figured it would pass, and I didn't dare tell anyone, for fear that they wouldn't let me go to that first workout. The season was only about two months away, and I figured it was because I had spent so much time in bed after the accident. I went on to the workout that day, but as I walked around the field, I kept losing my breath. I knew I was out of shape, but I couldn't have been that badly out of shape. After all, I had been in rehabilitation.

I first realized that I was in trouble as I drove home that night after the workout. I couldn't lift my right leg to go back and forth from the accelerator to the brake. I literally had to pick up my leg and move it with my hand. Once I got home, I was really having a hard time catching my breath. My mom and dad took me to the emergency room. The only thing I remember hearing was that I needed surgery.

When I came to, I was in a hospital room with my parents. Apparently, my appendix had ruptured, and they had to perform an emergency appendectomy. I was lying in my hospital room watching the July 4th fireworks out the window, staples all the way across my stomach, feeling very sorry for myself. I knew I wouldn't make it in time for football season. I thought I had a good reason for my pity party. This was the day after I got a doctor's release to play football. It was also when I realized that life wasn't fair. My parents didn't really care about the football thing. What I didn't know was that the doctors had lost my vital signs twice during the surgery. It never occurred to me that I had almost died.

I was determined to play. Once you miss your senior season, it's gone. I was not going to miss mine. Once I was given the okay to exercise, I did. One thing that I wasn't able to do was to throw very well. To be honest, as a quarterback, I never really had much of an arm anyway. I realized that I was not going to be the starting quarterback, so I had to find another way to get on the field. I had punted before when I was younger, but not yet in high school. I begged the coach in charge of kickers for a tryout. Not only did I try out, I also won the job. I had found my niche as a football player.

My leg was strong, and I worked hard to develop my form. I had a decent senior season, but I pulled a groin muscle halfway through the year. My season was far from good enough to earn a scholarship. My dad made some phone calls for me, and arranged for me to have the opportunity to try out at the University of Georgia. When I was a kid, I attended the Georgia Bulldog Football Camp every year. I grew up a Georgia fan, and wanted to play between the hedges. All I had to do was to be accepted at the university, and I would get my chance to play for the Dawgs.

What happened next was purely my own fault. I had already faced and beaten what was, in my opinion, my share of adversity. I thought it would be smooth sailing from there on. My grades in high school were not spectacular, but good enough to get me in. I needed to take the SAT, score at least the minimum required, and I was in. I figured it would be no problem. I didn't study or even take the practice test. As a matter of fact, I did nothing at all to research the test. All I knew was that they would practically give the points I needed on the test if I spelled my name correctly. Big mistake. I even guessed at the questions I didn't know. I figured guessing was better than leaving it blank. If you have taken the SAT, then you know that's a mistake. Lesson learned: *be prepared and never take anything for granted.*

Well you probably know what happened next. I got my test results, and I'm embarrassed to say that I missed the minimum requirement by thirty points. I had already graduated from high school, and the college camp was only a few weeks away. Since I had waited until the last minute to take the test, there wasn't enough time for a retake. My college dreams were fading fast, and there was no one to blame but myself. I had blown it.

Only God knows why certain events in our lives happen, and happen when they do. Everything happens for a reason. I also heard one time that "what doesn't kill us makes us stronger." I had experienced my disappointments, and I was beginning to wonder if I had set my goals too high. Maybe God didn't want me to play football beyond high school. I had run out of options, but I wasn't ready to quit yet. I searched for a school that would be willing to give me a tryout, but I couldn't find one. Then one night, it happened. I found my opportunity in what has to be the weirdest way.

My dad was reading the evening issue of the *Atlanta Journal* at the kitchen table and he yelled for me to come upstairs. He read me an advertisement about a college that was bringing back their football program. It had been some thirty years since they last participated in football, and they wanted to bring it back to the campus. All graduating high school players were invited for a tryout. I called the head coach, Ken Henry, the next morning, and scheduled the visit.

I was hesitant about giving it a try, and spoke to my parents about it the night before I left. What they said to me really changed my outlook on things. All they said was, "What do you have to lose? Are you worried about getting thrown off the team? You're not on it now anyway. Just go for it." I did, and signed to play for Tennessee Wesleyan College in August 1985. I had made it to the collegiate level. Now all I had to do was stay there. Little did I know, it would be a major undertaking.

2

The First Season

When I arrived in Athens, Tennessee, I was scared to death. I had no family in Tennessee, and as a matter of fact, I didn't know anyone in Tennessee, period. My parents drove me up for the start of camp and school, unloaded my things, and went home. After they left, I realized that I was on my own. It didn't take me long to realize how much I loved my mom, and how much I took her for granted. Let me give you an example. The first lesson I learned was that when I threw my clothes into a corner at the end of the day, they stayed there, and the pile grew every day. Somehow my clothes had forgotten how to wash themselves. Plus, my magic refrigerator was broken. No matter how many times I opened the door, the inside remained empty. I was used to opening the door and getting something to drink and eat. I was faced with the reality that I had to fend for myself. Boy, I missed my mom. If I could do it over again, I would definitely take my mom to college with me.

Once practice started, I didn't have the time or strength to do anything but football. To make matters worse, I didn't even punt one football. I was put with the defensive backs. This was a nightmare for me. I had played football my entire life, but never on the defensive side of the ball. See, I could take a lick with no problem, but when it came to delivering one, my life was in some real danger. I wasn't given the chance to punt because the school had signed a

9

kid from the local high school to punt. For publicity reasons, they felt that a local name would help sell tickets. Therefore, I was destined for the defensive backfield. Needless to say, I ended up last on the Defensive back depth chart. I did manage to make the kickoff team, so at least I was going to see the field.

The first game was billed as a big deal for the college. We were set to open against Emory & Henry College at home. It was our "sister" school, and the presidents of the two schools were friends. There were a lot of television and newspaper reporters there to cover the return of football to Tennessee Wesleyan College. The Defensive back coach told us that the first defensive back to get an interception in a game would get a steak dinner. I didn't get too excited about it, because I had pretty much no chance of getting in the game as a Defensive back, much less picking off a pass. The game started out as a disaster and didn't get any better.

It was late in the game, and we were down 62–12. Yeah, that score is correct. That's another lesson I learned. No matter what level of competition it is, high school or college, starting a program is painful. Anyway, it was late in the game, and we were getting killed, when the coach put me in at cornerback. After I got over the initial shock of being put in, I had to figure out how to survive. The first play went in the opposite direction from me, and I thanked God.

Then it happened. With time running out, the quarterback for Emory & Henry dropped back to pass. See, this was the worst-case scenario for me. I figured that if he ran my way, at least I would have help making the tackle, or at least I could slow him down a little. But no, they had to pass with a fifty-point lead, late in the game. I guess the presidents were not such good friends after all. I read the pass, and with my blazing 5.3 forty-yard speed, dropped to my zone, the whole time praying that they wouldn't throw over my head for a touchdown.

What happened next was purely the work of God's grace and protection. The quarterback threw to the tight end dragging across the middle. The ball was thrown kind of high, and it was tipped up in the air by the receiver. Instantly, my life and the game seemed to go in slow motion. I broke up on the ball and picked that baby off! I didn't run far, but after I went down, I realized that nothing was impossible. When I got to the sidelines, I could taste that steak dinner. Coach Newton didn't honor his end of the deal. His thinking was that the game was out of reach.

I felt sort of bad for the quarterback. He only added an interception to his stats with what was probably the worst defensive back to ever have played college football. As for me, I had gotten the first interception for the college in thirty years. I learned another important life lesson: stay with it and never quit; good things will happen.

I played in every game that season. Not at cornerback, but on the kickoff team. As a matter of fact, I don't think I ever got back in a game at cornerback the rest of the season. Our team finished 2 and 6 in the first season. All things considered, it wasn't as bad as it sounds. We were glad it was over. Next year, we thought, it would be better.

3

Something They Ate

During the off-season, I found out that the punter would not be returning to the college. I saw my opportunity and took it. I went to the head coach and begged him for the chance to punt. After all, that's what I was brought there to do in the first place. He gave me my opportunity, and by the start of the season, I was the starting punter. Little did I know that I would have to do more than punt later in the season.

My first season as a punter went pretty long. In the game against Millsaps College, I punted seventeen times. That was a record that even landed me on ESPN. I didn't get to see the newscast, but everyone at the school was talking about it that night. Apparently, the famous Chris Berman talked about the game and how many times I had to kick, calling me "Tony Punt-a-Lot-ti." All I know is that from that moment on, everyone on campus and off seemed to call me Tony PuntaLotti. Even the radio announcers for our games did it. That's not really how a football player wants to be remembered, but I guess it's better than nothing.

My other claim to fame that season was that I led the nation in roughing the punter penalties—also not quite the kind of notoriety a player wants. That season has to be the craziest season I ever played. It was about midway through the season, and we were getting ready to play Emory & Henry again, but this time at their place. We did not have a lot of depth at quarterback, so the coaches started getting me a little work in at practice. This was supposed to be for an emergency situation, a "just in case" kind of thing. Anyway, it was late in the game, and Emory & Henry was sticking it to us again, when the coach decided to play me at quarterback. His thought was: let's see what happens. Nothing major happened, except that the offense did move the ball and I even ran for a first down on a bootleg pass. We faked them out pretty good, but my blazing speed only allowed me to get about thirty yards before everyone was on me. This game would prepare me for what was yet to come.

I got more work in at practice running the offense during the next few weeks, and thank God, because I would need it. We were getting ready to travel to play Lambuth University in Jackson, Tennessee. I was listed as third string quarterback, especially when we were traveling. The night before we left, our starting quarterback went into a diabetic coma. He had a bad habit of hiding cupcakes and eating them late at night—not a smooth move for a guy who had to take two insulin shots every day. He turned out okay, but he wasn't able to make the trip. We went to Jackson with two quarterbacks, and I was one of them. It was to be a weekend I would never forget.

The number two guy knew he would have to play the whole game. Early in the first quarter, he was running with the ball and took a pretty good shot. He didn't get back up. I was told to get ready and take some snaps while the staff evaluated his injury. When I came off the field the next series, I was informed that he had separated his shoulder and was out for the rest of the game. I would have to kick and play quarterback for the whole game. I said a prayer and asked God to help me make it through the game.

Remember when I told you always to be prepared and how tough that lesson is to learn? I thought I had learned it, but apparently I hadn't. When you play quarterback, the smart ones wear rib protectors for added protection. I didn't bring mine, because it was too uncomfortable to kick in, and I didn't really think I would be playing quarterback. I took some good shots to my ribs, and after the game I found out that I had actually fractured one of them and badly bruised another. Ordinarily, you would think that this would be enough adversity for anyone to endure. My day was about to get much worse.

Have you ever heard the saying: "It can't get any worse"? I made the mistake of saying that, and after this game, I swore I would never say it again. You see, once you say that it can't get any worse…it usually does! Now I say, "It will only get so bad that, eventually, it has to get better!" I will never forget what happened next in this game.

I went into the huddle to call the play, and one of my linemen looked at me and said, "Lotti, I don't feel well. I don't feel like blocking." Not the phrase a quarterback wants to hear from his linemen. One after another echoed the phrase. "I don't feel well." It was late in the game when this started, and one by one, every player started getting sick. I tried to get substitutions for the sick players, but there was a problem. Players and coaches on the sidelines were getting sick. The illness was hitting one person after another, and we knew something was definitely wrong. The game finally ended, and we were all immediately put on the buses, and rushed to a nearby hospital, with a police escort.

The hospital staff greeted the bus and put disaster tags on all of us, coaches and trainers included. We had all contracted food poisoning. If you have ever been poisoned, you know that it is the worst experience next to dying you can have. I'll spare you the gory details. Being deathly ill is one thing, but to do it with bruised and broken ribs is another. I would not wish that misery on my worst enemy. I remember thinking that it was never going to end and praying that if I was going to die, then please, God, make it quick. Everyone with us on that trip got sick, including the bus drivers. We spent that night and part of the next day in the hospital.

Once the doctors released us to travel, we were taken straight to the hospital in our college town. Some of us had to be admitted there, yours truly included, due to severe dehydration. We even made the *USA Today* front-page headlines, in a story called "Something They Ate." For the next couple of weeks, every player had to meet in the auditorium about every other day, so that medical personnel could draw blood from us for analysis. They had to find out what made all of us sick. The talk was that the food poisoning came from a restaurant where we all ate while in Jackson, Tennessee. The college needed the proof, which explains all of the testing afterwards.

What happened next blew my mind. Everything stopped. No more testing, poking, prodding, or discussion about it. It wasn't until my parents received a hospital bill that the stuff hit the fan. Obviously, my parents refused to pay it, and they got together with other parents to find out what the deal was. We found out that our own school poisoned us.

Here's how. The day we left for Jackson, our cafeteria packed us food to eat on the way. That way, when we stopped to stretch our legs, we could eat. Everything would have been fine, except for the fact that the sandwiches were packed under the bus with all the equipment—yeah, nice move by the managers who packed the bus. Ham sandwiches do not keep very well when they are heated for hours by a transit bus's engine. The thing that bothered me the most was that the sandwiches didn't smell or taste funny. They were actually pretty good. I remember eating a couple myself. The managers didn't do it on purpose; heck, they got sick too. One thing I know for sure: I don't eat ham unless I prepare it. The school never packed us another snack for road trips during the rest of my career there.

The season was almost over, and for the last game of the season, we had to travel back to Jackson, Tennessee for the finale. Different opponent, same city. I had to start at quarterback and punt for the whole game again. No other quarterback made the trip. We almost pulled out the only victory of the season that day. We ended the season 0–10. We were glad that the season was finally over. Disappointed, we headed home from Jackson, tired and very hungry.

4

Improvise, Adapt and Overcome

I guess it was at this point of my college career that I strongly considered quitting. A lot of the guys had done just that. I would be lying if I said it didn't bother me, because it did. My grades were far from terrific, and my body was questioning whether this was really worth it. After my first two seasons, our record was 2–16. We didn't seem to be making any headway. During this off-season, Coach Henry was relieved of his duties. I liked Coach Henry, but I guess the school had to make a change. I will always be grateful to him, because he gave me a chance when no one else would. The college hired David Bankston to head up our program, and he would remain my college coach for the rest of my career.

Coach Bankston was a military guy who had previously coached at West Point. Let me tell you, there were a lot of times I thought I had left college and joined the military. His practices were like basic training. The thing that got me was the shape he was in. He did about all of the conditioning drills with us. I remember having to run as a team, and he was right there, running and singing. He would yell, "Jody, Jody, Jody, Jody!" I guess it was about a year later before one of us got up the nerve to ask him what the heck "Jody" meant. Since I had never officially joined the military, I didn't have a clue. Apparently, "Jody" is the term used by military personnel to describe the guy who stayed at home while you were defending your country—the guy who dated your girlfriend. Pleasant. huh?

The one thing you did not want to do was to break a team rule. If you did, that meant you earned a private conditioning program with Coach Bankston at 5:30 AM. I remember leaving the dorm for breakfast one morning (a team rule was that everyone had to attend breakfast every day) and there he was, running up the street with a misguided teammate. I'll never forget my teammate stopping to get sick and Coach Bankston jogging around him in circles, singing at him. When the player finished, they headed up the street and repeated the process for as far as I could see. I wasn't one to break team rules anyway, but now I was going to make darn sure I didn't. Life was tough enough; I didn't see any reason to bring something else on me.

The next two seasons were a huge improvement. I earned the starting punter position again, and ran the scout team offense at quarterback. We were winless going into the game against Camp-bellsville College during Bankston's second year, but we felt we had a good chance to pick up our first victory of the year. Usually, our Thursday practices were the last hard day of the week, and Friday was used as a game review. One Thursday after practice, Coach Bankston pulled me aside and asked if I had ever kicked field goals before. I told him that I had when I was little, but not in a very long time. He handed me some footballs and told me to get good at it fast. Our field goal kicker was also on a soccer scholarship, and the soccer team had made it into a tournament, so he wouldn't be in town for our game against Campbellsville. I had a night and a day to get ready to kick field goals in a game.

This high-pressure situation taught me a lot about life. Sometimes you don't know what is going to happen to you. Life is funny, throwing you curve balls and putting you on the spot from time to time. I called my dad that night to let him know. I remember hearing his voice on the phone say, "Wow, you guys have a real shot at winning this week, and you know, it will probably come down to a field goal." Thanks, Dad…like I wasn't already nervous. He was upset, because this was going to be the first game he and my mom would miss. They had to go to Boston to attend my cousin's wedding. He tried everything to get out of going, but was unsuccessful. You have to understand that my parents never missed one of my games, not even when I was little. They drove all over the country to see me play, and I appreciated it tremendously. It was so nice to be able to look at the stands and see at least two friendly faces. Dad would have to watch ESPN from Boston to catch the results this time.

It wasn't long into the game when I got my first shot at kicking a field goal in a college game. It wasn't a long one, only about thirty yards, but it was from the hash mark. It was so cool, because as soon as the ball was snapped, the game seemed to switch to slow motion. I made my approach to the ball and put everything into it. It seemed to launch from my foot. I knew I had hit it well. You can ask any kicker: they know if they have hit it well or if it's a shank. You don't even have to look up and see; you just know. The ball sailed straight down the middle of the uprights with plenty of room to spare. When the two officials put their hands in the air, signaling that the kick was good, it was one of the best sights I have ever seen. I went on to make my extra point after a touchdown, and even converted a two-point conversion after another. We ended up winning our first game of the season 32–29. Yes, a field goal decided it.

I couldn't wait to get back to the dorm room and call my dad. It was funny, because I had several messages to call him. I dialed my uncle's house, where they were staying, and the phone only rang once. My dad answered, saying, "What happened?" There's no telling how many other callers before me heard the same thing. I started off by asking if he had heard the news. He said no, he had been watching ESPN, but they hadn't run the score yet. See, there is a good reason for that. Usually, we got our butts whipped, and the winning team always jumped to report the score. Unfortunately, this was new for us, and the score hadn't been called in. I told my dad that we had won 32–29. His immediate response was, "You kicked a field goal, didn't you?" When I laughed at his response, he started yelling at my mom that it was her fault he had missed seeing it. I felt bad for my cousin, because they were all standing around when he said it. He would never see anything like it, because I never got another chance to kick a field goal again. The soccer player returned the following week. Unfortunately for him, though, when he missed a field goal, he heard it from my family in the stands.

In an Italian family, family is the most important thing, and it is believed that blood is always thicker than water. What that means, in a nutshell, is that you should never take sides with anyone over the family. Sometimes it is possible for the water to become so thick that it takes on the same qualities as blood. That is where my Aunt Linda and Uncle Jim come in. When we moved to Georgia from Boston, we were separated from my blood family. My parents met Aunt Linda and Uncle Jim a few months after we arrived, and they have been part of my family ever since. I remember times, when I was little, that Mom and Aunt Linda pooled their resources together so we could all eat. Aunt Linda and Uncle Jim have supported me in everything. They traveled with my parents to games, from the time I was little all the way to my last game in college. They will always be special to me and are an important part of our family.

5

The Choice

It's really strange how much I learned about life while I was in college. Life is full of choices, and it's funny how a wrong choice can be disastrous. I know the difference between right and wrong, and I have my parents to thank for that. Your parents raise you to know the difference between right and wrong, and they hope that the "home training" will kick in when it's needed. There is a lot of pressure to be successful in college athletics. A lot of emphasis is put on getting bigger, stronger, and faster. I also learned that everything has a price, and that the great rewards cost dearly.

I remember one night in my dorm room. A couple of players had gathered to hang out. My room was the hangout, because I had the only color television set. One of the guys went over and locked the door. He looked at the other guy, and said, "I got the stuff; are you ready?" I had no clue what he was talking about. Apparently, I was the only one that didn't. He was referring to the fact that he had gotten his hands on some anabolic steroids—testosterone, to be exact. Some athletes want to win so badly that they will do anything to achieve that competitive edge. I didn't share the same philosophy. See, to me, taking a drug to enhance your performance is not only cheating, but it also cheapens any accomplishment that you might reach. Let me explain. I told you that my secret goal and desire was to be named a collegiate All-American. To me, if I were to achieve that goal using drugs, then the title wouldn't mean anything, because I had cheated to get it. I wouldn't have earned it on my own. I chose to rely on my desire and God to reach my dreams, so that when I reached them, I could know that it was legitimate.

What I saw next confirmed to me that I had made the right choice. The guys who chose to use the drug did so by injection. From what I understand, injection gets the drug into the bloodstream quicker than taking it orally. Anyway, the needle looked huge and long. The person giving the shot simply stabbed the needle into the buttocks of the receiving player. I couldn't even watch. Later, there would be a huge bruise where the injection had been given. I knew I wanted no part of this process. All things considered, it didn't seem worth the risks involved.

You may be wondering how I could be in there and know which players were using and not be forced to participate. How could they be sure I wouldn't say anything? For starters, I was "just a kicker." No one really expected me to take part anyway. My teammates knew me. They knew that I wasn't a snitch. I believe that people are responsible for making their own decisions and are held accountable for their own actions. My upbringing told me that it was wrong, so when put in that situation, I chose to think for myself. That's a big part of life: choices. I don't believe in criticizing others for the decisions they make. God gave me a mind so I could think for myself, and I like to think it makes him happy when I use it. I am not saying I always make the right decisions, but I do hold myself accountable and no one else. In my opinion, that's the problem with most people today. Everybody wants to blame someone else for problems or misfortunes. If you don't like your life, then change it. You do have the power to take control and do something about it. Most people choose the easy way, and blame someone else. I choose not to.

Several months went by, and then I learned how correct my decision was. One of my teammates was using the bathroom after a workout and we heard him scream. While he was urinating, he had looked down to see that it wasn't urine, but blood. Another teammate's face swelled up to the point that he looked like you could stick him with a pin and he would explode. That was scary stuff. Again, I silently thanked my parents for giving me the strength to make the right decision. It was some time after this that mandatory drug testing was required for all football players. I think it's a great rule. I also think it is important to mention that the two players who decided to experiment with the stuff didn't last in college. They washed out after one season.

Another lesson I learned was about women. I learned that I will never figure them out, and that lesson lives on with me today. It is very hard to date when you're a football player in college. One big reason is that there is no time to date, and the other is that you're always broke. I'm in favor of paying college athletes. It doesn't have to be much, and it should be regulated so that there is a cap, and not the foolishly high figure given to professional athletes today. It can be done and should be. A college or university makes a lot of money from its sport programs. There is a tremendous amount of pressure put on college athletes, and the work is harder than any job I've had since my playing days ended. The bottom line is that dating was hard because you couldn't even afford to buy a girl a Big Mac, much less take her to a movie. Unfortunately, most girls don't enjoy just hanging out in the dorm and talking all the time.

I got what I guess you would call my first real girlfriend in college during my junior year. We ended up engaged to be married. We were good friends, and I enjoyed being with her, but she was a little possessive. I liked the idea of having a girlfriend, and I think I was more in love with the concept than actually in love with her. Toward the end of the relationship, I became interested in other girls and had no intention of setting a wedding date anytime soon. I was just going to have a good time, hopefully bring up my grades, and get ready for my final season as a collegiate football player. We were going to join the Mid-South Conference for my senior season, and I had a lot of dreams to reach, and not much time left to reach them. I had a busy summer of workouts scheduled and had to improve fast.

6

A Laugh or Two

During the summer before my senior season, I stuck to my workouts. I chose to stay in Athens again for the summer. That way I
could stay close to the school and work. I had been working in a
nightclub a couple of miles up from the school. For all intents and
purposes, it was a bar. The money was great, though. I started out as
a disc jockey, and was given the chance to be a bartender. That's
where the money is.

I kept a large bottle in my room at the house. Every night, I
would empty my quarters in the bottle. At the end of the week, I
would take the bottle to the bank. I never had less than a hundred
dollars in quarters each week. My roommate lived off my quarter tip
jar. As a college kid with a hundred dollars a week in quarters, I was
considered by my peers to be riding the gravy train. My roommate
and I used to sit up after I got in from work and count my tips. Not
counting the quarters, I would have a load of cash to go with it.

The best part was that I only worked three nights a week. Sure,
two of them were Friday and Saturday nights, but since I was making that kind of money, I didn't mind. The rest of my friends were
making about $3.45 an hour. I made more in four hours than they
did in a month. I would basically work and save all off-season, so
that I would have enough money to live during the season and not
have to work. Now, I won't go into a lot of detail about my bartend-

ing days. I could write a book on that experience alone. I will tell you this. It is true what they say about people telling all their problems to bartenders. I don't know why people think that bartenders are qualified to hear their problems. I guess it's because they have found the friendly face of someone who will listen.

People sometimes need someone to listen to them and not interrupt. I think that if you are going to call yourself a "people person," then you have to be a good listener. I learned a lot about life in that bar, and I have come to these conclusions. First of all, it doesn't matter how much money you do or do not have; there is always something else to bring you down. People who don't have money are down because they are broke and can't pay the bills. They want to be like that rich guy they see on the other side of the bar. "He has it made," they would say. "If I just had his money, I wouldn't have any worries." What they don't know is that the rich guy is miserable because he spends all his time making money and has no one in his life that cares about him. Sure, he has money, but that's about it. Money doesn't fix your problems. It eliminates the problem of not having any. But I promise, if you don't have a money problem, you'll have something else. Smile as much as you can, and roll with it, knowing that it's going to get better. If someone else's yard looks greener, it's probably not as green as you think.

Not only did I learn a lot about life in college, I had fun while learning. I sit back and think about different things we did. Some of them were pretty foolish, so here comes my disclaimer: don't try any of these things at home.

One of my teammates was simply a nut. You could never take this guy seriously, and you never knew what he was going to do next. His name was Tommy Bunch. Now, this guy was an ex-Green

Beret and had been a member of the Special Forces, and he was also a minister. What's wrong with this picture? Tommy had an old Ford Bronco that we used to pile in and hit the town. He would pull up next to a car on the highway, and when the folks in the other car would look over, he would scream at them. He never used profanity, or even words, for that matter; he'd just make faces and holler.

One time I was riding with him and two cops pulled up next to us and told Tommy to pull over. He knew he had been going a little fast, but do you think he pulled straight over? No, not Tommy. He put his head out the window and started screaming frantically at the officers that he didn't have any brakes. I leaned back in my seat thinking *Great, how am I going to explain this one to my dad from jail?* Bunch talked his way out of it. Bunch grew up in the next town, so apparently everyone knew he was crazy. Bunch was always pulling stuff. You never knew what was coming next.

Once, during a football game, a buddy of ours, Linder, made a late hit. The referee threw the flag. Well, when Bunch saw the penalty flag, he ran over to the referee and started telling him that the flag was unfair because Linder was deaf. Of course Linder was not deaf, but you have to picture Bunch pleading his case to the referee, waving his arms like he is doing sign language to Linder. I know where Bunch came up with this little scheme. See, during our freshman season, we traveled to play Galludet in DC. Galludet is a college for the deaf. Let me be the first to tell you that just because people can't hear doesn't mean they are not great athletes. Playing against them was another great moment in my career. Their campus was beautiful and first rate. I left wishing I went to school there. They had a big bass drum on the sidelines, and the coach would hit it for the snap count and things like that. You could feel the vibrations of that drum all the way to our sidelines. Talk about adapting and overcoming an obstacle; those guys did it. I received a huge blessing from that experience.

Oh yeah, we were penalized on that play. The referee didn't buy Bunch's explanation at all. I could go on and on with stories about my experiences with Tommy Bunch, but I won't. Okay, one more story.

We had a huge snowstorm one year at school. We were all outside messing around in it when Bunch showed up in the Bronco. He started telling us how fun it was to go sledding when there was a pretty good snow. Now, Bunch wasn't talking about the normal type of sledding. I guess a better term for it would be "redneck sledding." Bunch had a metal garbage can lid and a chain. He would tie the chain to the bumper of the Bronco and pull you around campus while you were sitting on the garbage can lid. Now, at face value, this sounded like a good time. After all, the place was covered with snow and ice, and it seemed like it would be fun. Well, I wasn't up for it, needless to say, but Tab decided he would give it a go.

Tab got situated on the garbage can lid, and the rest of us piled into the Bronco. The adventure for Tab started out fine. Bunch drove pretty slowly and pulled Tab around the campus. We were joking around and cutting up, when Bunch decided to speed up. Tab started yelling at Bunch to slow down, and Bunch—being Bunch—started yelling back at Tab, "What? Speed up? Okay!" and he did just that. Then Bunch pulled out onto one of the side streets, and Tab was holding on for dear life. The speed of the Bronco wasn't necessarily the problem. The problem was that the road had been cleared of snow and Tab was riding on nothing more than pavement. Do you know what happens when metal is dragged across pavement? That's right—a little phenomenon called friction occurs. Friction produces heat, and that's not good. Sparks were flying out from underneath the garbage can lid and Tab was still holding on. We all started yelling at Bunch to stop, and he made a hard turn. All we saw was Tab being slung around behind the Bronco, hitting a curb, and disappearing into the darkness of someone's yard.

We stopped and ran over to find Tab holding his backside. The heat had burned right through his pants, and he was standing there exposed to the elements in that spot only. The garbage can lid was burnt straight through. Once we saw that Tab was okay, we began to laugh hysterically. Now, come on, you can picture him standing there with his rear end exposed. It was funny, but an extremely stupid stunt on our part. I'm sure that Bunch would still say he thought Tab wanted him to go faster and that he thought the road had snow on it, but we all know Bunch better than that.

Another teammate and close friend that I have to tell you about is John D. John D. was the type of guy that everyone liked. He was a pretty big guy who played on the line for us. He was as easygoing as anyone you'll ever meet. He and I moved off campus for our last two years, along with Pike (another lineman). The strange thing about this living arrangement was that you had two linemen living with a punter. Usually, linemen do not associate with kickers. Why? I don't know; it's just the way it is. Later on in life, I was at a business meeting with Jeff Merrow. Jeff had been a defensive lineman and had an awesome career with the Atlanta Falcons. We stopped for dinner one night after our meeting, and he looked at me and said, "Hey, Lotti, know what? This is the first time I've ever eaten with a kicker." We laughed, and then he said, "Don't tell anyone about it." He probably doesn't even remember me now.

John D. and I rented a three-bedroom farmhouse off campus which later became known as the Ponderosa. That's right; this place came fully equipped with cows and everything. Many legends and some lies came out of the Ponderosa. We developed a close relationship with some girls from town and became very good friends. I know what you're thinking, and no, we were just close friends. I will tell you that the girls we did date didn't seem to like them, though. Angie and Lolly will always be special, because of the times we had. It was pretty common for us to play jokes on each other. I'll give you an idea of what I mean.

John D. and I had a washing machine, but not a dryer. In college, you never did the laundry until it was absolutely necessary. If you went off to college, you know I'm speaking the truth. I mean, you were down to wearing the last stitch of clothing found in the drawer. Anyway, we did the laundry and hung the clothes out to dry. We went to football practice, and when we pulled up in the driveway, I thought John D. was going to bust a gasket. Every piece of clothing was gone from the clothesline, with the exception of one piece. A pair of John's boxer shorts was hanging on a pole at the end of our driveway. I tried not to laugh, for fear of my life, but I couldn't help it. We called Angie and Lolly, and of course they knew nothing about it. They did, however, happen to find our clothes, and they brought them back.

My teammates and I were all good friends and were very close. We would pick at each other and do some pretty goofy things together, but understand one thing: we would do anything for each other. If someone from the outside messed with one of us, they had to deal with all of us. We are a family, and I would do anything for these guys. We joke about it now and reminisce about the different times we shared during those days. One thing will never change: to this day, if one of them needs me, for whatever reason, I'll be there.

7

A Season to Remember

The time had finally come for my last season in college. We had high hopes that this would be the season in which our team would be successful. There were only four of us left from freshman year: Tab Carpenter, John Linder, Scott Mason, and myself. The four of us lasted through a college career that was filled with nothing but adversity. We were fifth-year seniors and had only had four wins in the past four years. The question always seemed to come up with everyone, including reporters: "Why have you stayed?" The four of us saw a lot of players come and go, but we chose to stick it out. Don't get me wrong, there were many times we thought about hanging it up. We couldn't. It wasn't in us to quit. We were not raised that way. My dad used to say that once you quit the first time, the rest of the times are easy. As I mentioned earlier, I was never allowed to quit anything once I started. These guys had the same mentality.

In my opinion, this is the secret to becoming a champion in life. Whatever the circumstance or endeavor, one key ingredient in all champions is perseverance. If you work hard enough, believe hard enough, and persevere through the hard times, you can realize your dreams.

Our first game of the year was on the road against Georgetown. They were a powerhouse in our conference, and had been picked to win it all this year. We went up there and played hard, but got blown out 42–6. I kicked well, but we were all pretty disappointed in the outcome of this first game. We knew that this year would be different.

Week after week, the losses continued to mount up. Despite the fact that the team wasn't doing too well, I continued to kick well and often. Toward the end of the season, we were getting ready to play the University of Evansville. They were favored big in this game, but there was a side game of sorts going on for this one. Their punter and I were battling for the top punting slot in the Mid-South Conference. Our coaches decided to break this news before the first day of practice that week. Each day, the coaches would count down to the big game: "Five days to Wapner," and so on. Come Saturday, the judge would be in to determine who had the best punting unit. For those of you who don't know who Judge Wapner is, he was on a television show called "The People's Court." There was also a movie, "Rain Man," in which Dustin Hoffman would count down, saying, "Five minutes to Wapner." He didn't want to miss the show, and the coaches thought no one should miss this one either. We took pride in our punting unit. What was so special about it was that all four of us were on it. Linder snapped it, I kicked it, and Mason and Carpenter covered it. Carpenter also caught all three of my passes on fake punts for first downs.

I have to admit that I was nervous going into this game. Players would always get "butterflies" in their stomachs before playing, but this was worse. Everyone made a big deal of this match-up between their punter and me. For your information, in order for a punter to be considered for All-American, he must win the conference punting title. Each coach in the conference votes for the player who should be named the best. The punting title was on the line. Even Greg Vandagriff, who was back deep to return the other team's punt, came up to me before the game. "I will catch everything today," he said. "He won't get any rolls to help his average." This made me realize that this was important to the team. Realizing my dream of being an All-American is an individual award, but accomplishing it was definitely a team effort.

I knew that the first punt would set the tone for the other kicker to follow. Funny...the night before the game, my dad told me the same thing. "Look at it this way," he said. "Whoever gets to kick first can put the pressure on the other guy. You'll probably be first, so make it a good one!"

Me with
Mike McDonald
giving protection

The day was finally here. Pre-game warm-ups went pretty well; I was hitting the ball well. The game started with us kicking off, so it looked as if the other guy might get the first chance. We actually recovered the opening kickoff and went down and kicked a field goal to take an early lead, 3–0. We kicked off to them again, but from their first play from scrimmage, they completed a 64-yard pass for a touchdown to take the lead 7–3. We received the next kickoff, and the offense stalled out bringing up fourth down. Here it was: I would get the first kick.

It's funny how nervous I was when I first ran out there, but once I got behind the center, everything went silent. I couldn't hear the crowd, or anything else, for that matter. I just relaxed and focused. Everything was tuned out. The snap was a good one, and I went through the motion and kicked it. I knew I had hit a good one. All athletes know when they have done it right; maybe you have heard them talk about being "in the zone." I knew, when the ball hit my foot, that I had hit it cleanly and well. It turned over and went forty-nine yards. Today, I was in the zone. The thought process was correct. The pressure was on him now, and his first punt wasn't very good: only about thirty-five yards.

I knew it wouldn't be long before I got another chance, and I was right. It's funny, but I remember it well. As usual, Linder gave me a good snap, and I hit it well. The ball took off in a tight spiral and turned over. The protection was great with my upback, Mike McDonald, blocking the only threat. I went on to punt ten times in that game and carried a 46-yard average. Evansville's punter only averaged about thirty-four yards that day. I took sole possession of the conference lead and never lost it.

When the final conference standings came out, I was sitting on top with eighty-one punts for a 41-yard average. Each coach has a vote for players being named All-Conference. Coach Bankston later told me that I was named first team All Mid-South Conference and had received top votes from all the other coaches in the conference as well.

1989 Dad, Me & Mom after Georgetown game

With the announcement of the All-Conference team, there was nothing to do but wait for the All-America list. I didn't know whether or not my season stats were strong enough to make it. My dad told me not to worry about it. I'd had a great season and there was nothing else I could do about it at this point. That's another subtle but great lesson I got from my dad. "Don't worry about what you can't control," he would say. I try to live by that to this day. If you stop and think about it, it's sound advice.

Even though my dad spoke with a carefree tone, I knew he was sweating the news as much as I was. Usually, according to what I was told, the association only takes the top five punters in the country and makes them All Americans. I didn't know whether, by stats alone, my case was strong enough. Then, finally. the news came. Coach Bankston sent word that he wanted to see me in his office. When I got there, he called me in and smiled. "Congratulations," he said, and handed me a sheet of paper. On it were the final standings for all punters in the nation. I was ranked fourth. The funny thing about it was that I had punted fifty times more than any other punter ranked in the top ten. There was only about three yards in the averages that separated me from the top spot. I was in the top five and happy, not just for me and my family, but also for my teammates and my college. After a winless season, this was something everyone could be proud of. After all, if it hadn't been for them, it wouldn't have been possible.

From no chance to collegiate All American. What a ride!

1989 All American
All Mid South Conference

8

The Importance of Communication and Gatorade

Once the news of being named an All-American was released, things got pretty hectic. I have to admit that the attention was nice, though. My life began to change. I had a secret crush on a girl at the school, a cheerleader, but I couldn't tell anyone. After all, I was engaged to someone else at the time. I just couldn't help myself. She was so beautiful, and I found myself going places that I wouldn't normally go to, just so I could run into her. It's funny, but I remembered something my dad had told me on one visit home. I was stressing out about my relationship, and about whether or not I was really supposed to marry this girl. My dad simply said, "You haven't met the girl you're supposed to marry yet." He was right as usual, because I had found the one. The trick would be to convince her.

One night, we were having a surprise party for my roommate John D. What caught me off-guard was that Debbie showed up. She never went to any parties at the school, so I figured this had to be fate. I finally got up the nerve to go over and talk to her. I won't go into the details of the conversation, but let's just say it was short and didn't go as I had planned. I believe the term would be "crash and burn." I walked off, thinking that I knew she was the one, but she sure didn't.

I refused to give up on her, though. I was invited to a professional camp out in Nevada. When I returned, some people were having a get-together, and I figured I would make an appearance. To my surprise, Debbie was there. I didn't dare go over to her again, but what happened next blew my mind. She started to make her way over to me. Now I was feeling good about myself, thinking *I'm the man.* As she approached, I began to think of all the great things she would say to me. "I'm glad you're back. I really missed you. I need to tell you that I'm madly in love with you." My mind kept making it up as she walked over. When she finally made it over to me, she said, "Hi, Tony. Kelley wants to know if you will dance with her." Now, I'm sure I made the stupidest face when she uttered those words. I thought to myself, *You've got to be kidding me.* My mind raced to come up with a smooth line, a comeback. I didn't want to dance with Kelley; I wanted to dance with Debbie. So out it came: probably the corniest line ever, but I panicked. I said, "No, I don't want to dance with her, but I do want to dance with you." Well, it worked, because she said, "Okay." After that, I knew my life would never be the same.

We talked afterward, and I was sure she was the one. The next day, I broke up with my other girlfriend. Debbie was the one for me.

A special ceremony was being held for me back home in Clayton County, Georgia. I was receiving proclamations that declared February 24, 1990 was "Tony Lotti, Jr. Day." I asked Debbie to be my date for the event, and she said she would. Now would come the real test: she would meet my family.

Me & Debbie
Senior Banquet - TWC

At the ceremony, I was very surprised to receive my All-American ring. I hadn't thought it would be ready in time for the ceremony. What made it extra-special for me was that my grandmother was the person to present it to me. I had played football for my whole life, and my grandparents had never seen me play. When I was a little boy, Nana would tease me that she was going to run on the field in the middle of a play, screaming, "Tippy, it's hot, you need your Gatorade!" "Tippy" is my family nickname, and as you can imagine, I was terrified that my friends might find out that fact. I would be teased forever.

During my freshman year at college, I received a phone call telling me that my grandpa had passed away. The coaching staff told me that I didn't have to play in the game the next day. I told them that I wanted to play, because I knew in my heart that he would finally be there in spirit. In my very last game in college during my senior year, I got the surprise of my life. We were in pre-game warm-ups, and I was close to the sidelines, when I heard a voice from the crowd holler, "Tippy!" I looked over to the first row of stands, and there was a little old lady holding a small paper bag. It was my Nana, oxygen tank and all. I went over to her, and she passed me the small paper bag. "Do you want to guess what is in this?" she asked. I didn't even have to look in the bag. It was by far the best drink of Gatorade I had ever had.

I wear my All-American ring every day. It serves as a daily reminder that I should never give up on my dreams, no matter how unattainable they may seem. It also reminds me of the struggle to get there, and of the guys that actually made the dream become a reality: my teammates. I owe it all to them. Mason, Carpenter, Linder, Bunch, Tabor, McDonald, Vandagriff, Woods and the rest of my teammates will always have my highest respect and thanks.

Debbie comes from a small country-type family. My family is a big, typical Italian family. Two worlds would definitely collide at this ceremony. I could tell she was nervous about meeting everyone. I even had family visiting from Boston. She was going to be thrown into the deep end. We had to make a stop at the elementary school I attended, so some pictures could be taken of me with some of my previous teachers. Debbie was going to hang out with some of my family members during the shoot. While I was getting my pictures taken, I noticed everyone laughing. I looked at Debbie, and her face was turning red. I thought to myself, *Uh-oh.*

Communication between people is very important. Unfortunately, even though we all speak the same language, sometimes the words don't mean the same thing to everyone. Let me explain.

My Uncle George, who is from Boston, was trying to make conversation with Debbie. Debbie and I had driven straight from school in Tennessee to the elementary school in Georgia where the pictures were to be taken. My uncle asked her, "So how long have you been driving?" Of course he wanted to know how long it took us to get to the school from Tennessee. Well, Debbie's response was, "About four years." She was pretty nervous, and took his question to mean how long she had had her license. The family got a good laugh at it, and yes, Debbie was embarrassed. Miscommunication would define the family's relationship with her for some time.

Debbie and I started dating seriously from then on. We would joke about setting a wedding date. One night, at my house off-campus, we picked September 15, 1990 as a wedding date. Later, I would talk to Debbie's parents and ask their permission. Once I received their blessing, I got down on one knee and asked her to marry me in her mom's kitchen. She said "yes," and it was official. Her parents, and mine for that matter, freaked out when they found out it would happen in a few months. That's why I got a "yes" from them before I gave them the "when."

I signed with Professional Kicking Services (PKS) in Nevada. This is the premier agency for kickers in the NFL. I was on my way. The next several months would have me traveling all around the United States attending training sessions to make an NFL team.

What happened to me next is another life lesson. *Always finish what you start.* I had started college with the intention of earning a degree. With all the excitement of a career in the NFL, I lost focus on my graduation. I wasn't attending classes because of the air travel to camps, and I failed some of my courses during the last semester before graduation. When graduation day came, I was one one-hundredth of a point away from the graduation requirement. I was not going to graduate with my class as planned.

Everyone tried to talk Debbie and me out of getting married once this happened. They said that we didn't know each other well enough to get married. I think they used this as an excuse, but were really thinking that I should try to graduate first. I was so embarrassed about not graduating that I decided to return home to Morrow, Georgia and look for work. We were still planning to get married on September 15, with or without a degree.

I still had not been able to reach my final dream of getting to an NFL team, but by this point, I didn't care. I wasn't going to give up. Despite the hardships, all was good. I was getting the girl of my dreams.

Me & Debbie - Senior Formal - TWC

9

Pack the Bags—We're Going to Training Camp

Once home, I began to go to job interviews. After all, it was mid-August and I was getting married in less than a month. I was still working out and kicking the football. I wasn't going to give up on my dream of making it to an NFL team.

I had a job interview with a radio station out in Newnan, Georgia one morning. The interview went well, but all they could offer me was a part-time position. That wouldn't work, because I had to have something full time. Dejected, I left the interview and drove back to my mom and dad's house. When I pulled into the driveway, my mom came out the front door and asked, "How did the interview go?" Before I could answer her, she said, "It doesn't matter. Come inside now." As I entered the house, I could hear her screaming for my dad. "He's home! Hurry and get in here!" I asked her what the problem was, but she would only say, "Your dad has something to tell you." My dad came in and gave a little laugh, as if to drag on the suspense. "What? What do you want?" Finally, my mom told him that if he didn't tell me now, then she was going to do it. Dad looked at me and asked, "How did the interview go?" My mom was ready to kill him. He started laughing, and told me that the New England Patriots had called, and they were bringing me into training camp. I asked him when, and he said that my flight would leave that evening. I couldn't believe it. I was ecstatic.

The call I had waited for my whole life had finally come. It wasn't just the NFL—it was the Patriots. I hurried to pack my bags and make phone calls. Of course I called Debbie, who was back in Tennessee.

My family was very excited, and even though he didn't say anything about it, I could see the joy on my dad's face. He drove me to the airport for my flight that night. I knew he was proud. When I arrived in Providence, Rhode Island, a staff member of the team greeted me. Since it was late, he took me to my dorm room at the Patriots training facility. Once in my room, he told me to get a good night's sleep and he would wake me in the morning for practice and a meeting with the coaching staff. No way was I going to get any sleep that night; I couldn't settle down from the excitement.

The next morning, I ate with the team. Lord have mercy, it was the greatest spectacle of food I had ever seen in my life. Of all the great experiences in training camp, the one that I will never forget is the food. Buffet style all the way, baby! Whatever you wanted, it was there. For lunch, there was a hot bar, cold-cut (deli meats) bar, bread bar and literally, if you could eat it, it was there. There was even a Jell-O bar. If it was a color, it was on the Jell-O bar. You could eat all you wanted. This was very impressive to a small-time kid hanging out in the big league.

After we had eaten, I was taken over to the head coach's office. The Patriots had a new head coach that season named Rod Rust. I met him and some of my childhood idols that were assistant coaches. I met Steve Nelson, and then probably one of the biggest men I had ever met, Bruce Armstrong. Armstrong was an All-Pro offensive tackle and had a massive build.

Joe Mendez, the director of player personnel for the Patriots, took me out to the fields for practice. On the field, I was introduced to Gannons, the long snapper. He was massive too, and could snap the ball back to you so fast that if you didn't get your hands up to catch it, it would put a hole in your chest. Then Mr. Mendez saw a player walk by and yelled at him to come over and meet me. I froze in my steps. It was Steve Grogan.

As I mentioned earlier in this book, I have been a Patriots fan since I could talk. One day, when I was a kid, my dad took me to the Patriots training camp. We got to meet the players and get some autographs. Steve Grogan was in his rookie season. He came over to me and started up a conversation. I didn't say much; after all, I was pretty much in awe. He agreed to have his picture taken with me, and he became my football hero from that moment on. I even changed my football jersey number to the number *14* because of him. Those few moments he spent with me meant the world to a big-eyed kid. Now I walked onto the practice field with my hero. We shared a brief conversation, and at the risk of sounding like a star-struck rookie (which I was), I told him the story of how we first met. He was beaten up from all the years of playing in the NFL, and when he realized how we had first met, he laughed and said there was no way he was that old. He was, in my mind, not only a hero, but a warrior. No matter what happened from this point on, despite my disbelief, I had done it. My impossible dream had become a reality.

My career with the Patriots would be short, but sweet. I got the chance to have my impossible dream come true. Signing autographs for fans and kids was an awesome experience. Being told to report to the head coach's office is the last thing any player in training camp wants to hear. For them, it's the equivalent of the phrase "dead man walking." No player ever wants to report the head coach's office. It is that simple. Sure enough, when I got there, I heard "Taps" in my head, and I knew it was time to awaken. I was handed a plane ticket and sent home. They did feed me my "last meal" and take me to the airport. I would have gotten my chance to play against the Cincinnati Bengals the next night, but it wasn't meant to be. Once I took my seat on the Delta jet, the pilot informed us over the loudspeaker that the plane would be late taking off. "We are sorry for the delay," he said. "We just brought in the Cincinnati Bengals for their game against the Patriots, so we'll need extra time to restock the plane." Well, that was all it took for me. The tears just started coming. That was the longest flight home in my life.

I have mixed emotions about my experience with the Patriots. One side of me is proud and thankful that I made it that far. I should be happy that I made it farther than most guys do, but that just doesn't seem to sit well. I was even called up by the Atlanta Falcons for a private tryout, but that didn't go over well either. I punted the ball very well in my tryout with Atlanta, but I guess it just wasn't in God's plan for me to get a full year's contract and actually play in a game. I think the reason it still hurts to this day that I didn't make the roster in New England is that I wasn't at my best in practice. I was nervous all the time and just didn't play the way I knew I could. When you do your absolute best, you can always live with the outcome. That's the message I want people to get. Take advantage of every opportunity, and always bring your "A" game in everything you do. There is no doubt in my mind that if I had punted in New England the way I did for the Falcons, I would have played in that game against Cincinnati. It's hard to reach for that impossible dream against improbable odds, have it finally in the palm of your hand, and not be able to fully close your hand around it. I was blessed to reach my dreams, and I learned a valuable life lesson in the process. Your best is all you can ever give, so make sure you give your best effort in everything you do. Only then can you move on with no regrets.

10

Life Lands a Sucker Punch

Another lesson I would learn is that nothing lasts forever. The old saying that "success is a journey, not a destination" is probably one of the most accurate things I have ever read. The point that you have to understand is that life itself is a journey. There are ups and downs. The good and the bad of it is that neither one of the two last forever. I had been riding high for a while, with the All-American season and going to the Patriots. I came to a point in my life when it was time to test my inner will again. I came crashing down hard. The season was now in full swing, and I hadn't been picked up by another NFL team. I had just gotten married, and my savings were almost gone. I desperately started to search for a job, and things kept getting worse. Since it was late in the year, just about everyone had hiring freezes on. The interviews that I went to brought nothing but more frustration. I was desperate. One place even told me I was overqualified. I hadn't realized there was such a thing.

One day, while searching the want ads, I came across an ad looking for people with athletic backgrounds. There was even an emphasis on prior football-playing experience. The ad didn't go into a lot of detail, but they wanted potential applicants to submit a resume at a convention center in Atlanta. I was pretty excited about this opportunity and figured it was with a company associated with football or football equipment.

I went down to the convention center on the day indicated, dressed in a suit, carrying a great attitude. There were several people there, so a man addressed all the applicants at once. He began to talk about the great opportunities offered by Waffle House. At first I figured that I hadn't heard him correctly, but then he said it again. This was a job fair for Waffle House. I was pissed, to put it bluntly. I felt that I had been deceived. What in the world does working at a Waffle House have to do with having playing experience in football? My first thought was to get up and leave—after all, I had gotten sucked into every money-making scam under the sun, and to me, this was another one. I didn't leave. I decided I was going to wait until the end and give the guy a piece of my mind. When he finished speaking, I went up to him and asked him if I could have a word with him. I told him that I felt deceived by their advertising practices, because all they mentioned was athletic experience and never once mentioned the name Waffle House. I asked him, "What in the world does having playing experience in football have to do with Waffle House?" What he said blew my mind.

He replied, "Waffle House is one of the most successful businesses in America. The reason we recruit former athletes to our management program is because we have found, in studying employee pools, that people who come from an athletic background and participated in football tend to make the best employees. These athletes are used to playing for a team and dedicate themselves to the team philosophy. Those are the people we want to hire, and that is what contributes to our success." He might have been filling me a line of bull, but when I stopped to think about it, it really made pretty good sense. Either way, in my mind, I wasn't going to work in a Waffle House. I took his contact information and left.

Debbie and I then found out she was pregnant with our first child. This was truly one of the happiest days in my life. The day after brought the panic. I had a new wife who was now pregnant. I didn't have a job, which also meant that I didn't have any medical insurance. I had to find a job, and quick, so I bit the bullet and called the guy from Waffle House. During our conversation, he said he wanted me to come up with a required salary figure. I called him the next day and threw a figure at him of $35,000 a year to start. Back in 1991, that was a pretty good starting salary for someone with no real work experience. Plus, I figured he would say "no," and that would get me off the hook. While we were going over my "list of demands" for working there, he started bumping my figures up. He would say, "You'll need more money for this, and for that," and when he finished, he was giving me about $42,000 a year. Totally surprised, I accepted, and went to work for Waffle House.

I couldn't seem to get over the stereotype of what it meant to work at a Waffle House. I even asked if I could start at a store that wasn't local; that way I wouldn't run into anyone I knew. I wouldn't even wear the Waffle House shirt until I got to the restaurant. I was afraid I would see someone I knew at a traffic light and they would notice the shirt. Even when I would run into someone I knew and they would ask what I was doing (since I wasn't playing ball), I would tell them that I was still looking rather than tell them I worked there.

Let me stop right here and clear up some things concerning Waffle House and its employees. In all my years, I have yet to meet a nicer, harder-working group of people. It is, by far, the cleanest restaurant I have ever been in. The food is always fresh, because there are never any leftovers that sit in a freezer. Fresh food is brought in every morning. The other thing I noticed is that you literally meet all different types of people there, from a guy who is down on his luck and only has enough money for a cup of coffee to executives of multi-million-dollar companies. Everyone eats at a Waffle House. I think every person should have to spend some time working at a Waffle House. I promise that you will not complain about your current job, no matter what that might be. You flat work your tail off there. The people there, they're special.

I wasn't cut out to have a career at the Waffle House. I remember one night in particular. It was New Year's Eve, and I had to stay for the late shift. I was already tired from working my regular shift. So you know, a manager there is required to work a minimum of fifty-five hours a week. That's six days on and one day off. My only day off was Wednesday.

It was after two o'clock in the morning when I was called to the bathroom area. Someone who had had too much to drink, got sick all over the place. I'll spare you the details. Forced to clean it up myself, I sank into what I determined to be the lowest point in my life. I had decided that this was rock bottom: broke, and cleaning the bathroom at a Waffle House on New Year's. I began to tell myself that this was what my life has come down to. I would be lying if I didn't say I honestly thought about ending this misery. How did I fall so far so fast? I literally went from signing autographs for kids to cleaning a toilet at a Waffle House in a matter of weeks. It all happened so fast that I lost all control. The worst part was that I didn't know how. With an insurance policy, I was worth more dead than alive. I remember thinking that Debbie and the baby would be better off without me. I had all the pressures of a new wife and a new baby, and I was failing miserably. I felt like my wife's parents were probably looking at me as white trash; after all, I had taken their daughter away with big hopes and dreams that had materialized into being broke and scrubbing toilets.

I drove home the next morning in tears, partly because I was tired and extremely frustrated. On the way home, I considered crossing the middle line a few times. I even thought of driving right off a bridge. I began to talk to God—out loud! "Why are you letting this happen?" I asked. I felt like God began to speak to me. Up until now I was being a man. What was I ashamed of? I was doing whatever it took to take care of my family. That's being a man. Thinking about quitting and leaving my baby was not. It was like God told me to suck it up and keep going—it wouldn't last forever. He was right, as always. A few days later, I received a call for an interview with the gas company. It was an entry-level warehouse job, but I didn't care. I took it.

I also continued to do whatever it took to finish my degree at Tennessee Wesleyan. I finally got my bachelor's degree in 1993. I received my degree in the mail—no fancy graduation parties or robes, just an envelope in the daily mail. I still regret the fact that my parents never got to see me wear the cap and gown. I know it bothered my dad that I hadn't attended the graduation ceremony, but the main thing was that I finished what I started and did graduate. One thing is for sure: I did it the hard way. To this day, I am grateful for all that Tennessee Wesleyan did for me. Some people knock going to a smaller school, but it was a great experience for me. I learned more from that school than book knowledge. The faculty and community there are special people. My time at Tennessee Wesleyan had its ups and downs, but it is still one of the best times of my life. I didn't know it then, but God knew what he was doing when he put me there.

I busted my tail and worked my way up to a management position with the gas company. It took five years of working hard, volunteering in other departments to cross-train, and doing whatever it took. I was promoted to manager of the NGV Information Center in 1996. I was also appointed manager of the American Gas Association's sponsorship of the 1996 Olympic Games in Atlanta. I was making a very nice salary, and I had a big office, a company car, and people working for me. I had two beautiful little girls, Antonia and Anissa, when Debbie gave me my third precious gift. In 1997, my son, Anthony, was born. My kids are three good reasons I will never think about quitting again, no matter what happens down the road. Everything was going great, and I felt that I was where I was supposed to be. I was somebody again, and I had God and the Waffle House to thank for it.

11

The Billboard

I'll repeat the phrase: "Success in life is a journey, not a destination." In my mind, I was back up again. You have to hang in there through the rough and terrible times, knowing that sooner or later the sun is going to come back out. Just as the sun doesn't always shine, it doesn't rain forever, either. You have to keep fighting. Enjoy the good times, and buckle down during the bad. Neither one will last forever.

I had put in about nine years at the gas company, but had been miserable for the last two. The company had changed drastically. A lot of great people had been let go, and no one was happy with the new management. I was under a lot of pressure to cut employees in my department in an effort to reduce the head count. There was no long-term benefit to doing that in my department, but upper management was more concerned with the short-term results for shareholders. As a salaried employee, I was expected to be available 24/7. The bonus program was cut, and I gave up the company car to reduce expenses for my department, but nothing seemed to make it work. My health had even begun to suffer. I went back to school to study for a real estate license. After getting my license, I began to practice real estate part time. The gas company was our only form of income, and since Anissa and Anthony had joined the family, I figured I had better start "moving some eggs into another basket." It became obvious to me that I wouldn't retire from the gas company, so to me it was a smart idea.

My part-time income in real estate started to surpass my full-time wages at the gas company. I kept having pains in my stomach, and I finally had to break down and go to the hospital. Debbie found me on the kitchen floor one morning and made me go. I ended up having to have emergency surgery to repair my stomach and remove my gall bladder. Apparently, my gall bladder decided to stop working. Once again, the doctors said I was lucky, because had it gone on any longer, it would have gotten worse and caused me some major problems. The doctors recommended that I find another line of work. The stress from the situation at the gas company was taking its toll on me. I wrote out my resignation on New Year's Day, but didn't have the guts to turn it in. Once again, I began to pray.

I was scared to death to resign from a salaried job to move into a commission-based career where I was self-employed. I agonized, until one night, in desperation, I asked God to please give me a billboard telling me what to do. "I know you don't usually give us a billboard, but please give me one this time." I begged God for help.

The next morning I got a call telling me to come to a management meeting downtown. Driving there, I had the feeling that my life was getting ready to change. During the meeting, it became apparent that my career there had come to an end. My boss felt that it was time for new leadership in my department, and I agreed. I handed him my resignation, and that was that.

The guy I reported to had what you would call a "little Caesar" complex. This refers to a man who is, shall we say, "height-challenged." If you have ever worked in an office, you might have run into this type of boss. I even heard people refer to him as "Napoleon." Now, don't misunderstand me—there was nothing physically or genetically wrong with this guy; he was just short. (I'll give him the benefit of the doubt and say he was five-foot-five.) Sometimes people like this become bosses, and this guy had a complex, but not all do.

The company set this relationship up to fail, because they had me, a manager, reporting to another manager. who we'll call "Big T." (By the way, I'm 6'1"). I'll spare you the history lesson, but I'll say we were in rival departments that the company decided to merge together. It was destined to fail. It's funny, but I made the huge mistake of telling Big T that I was going to resign. Stupid mistake on my part. I should have followed the family rule: never let anyone know what you're thinking. My secretary, whom I really looked after, pulled a "Fredo" on me, and between the two of them, my hand was forced. So you know, the term Fredo comes from the *Godfather* movies where a brother, named Fredo, betrays his family.

I left the meeting downtown, but before I did, Big T commented to me that I sure was taking it real well. I looked at him, smiled, and said, "You think you had something to do with today's outcome, but you didn't. Today I received my billboard." He wanted to talk to me further. He said it bothered him to have someone out there that didn't like him. All I told him was, "You reap what you sow in this world, and what goes around comes around." Remember those two sayings. If you don't believe in anything else, believe them. The Bible guarantees it. It doesn't matter what you do in this world, this fact will always remain. The plus and minus to it all is that it always comes back to you in a greater magnitude than the way you sent it. Do good things for people without expecting things in return, and you will receive your blessing. Screw people over, and you will get screwed even worse. Sometimes it takes a long time to see it come back, and sometimes you may never even know that it did. Trust me: sooner or later, it comes back.

I guess it was a few months later when my phone began to ring off the hook. The calls were all from people at the gas company asking me if I had heard the news. Apparently, Big T had showed up for work one morning, and security was waiting for him. He had been told that he was no longer needed, and had been escorted from the building. I know he never saw it coming. He had thought that one day he would be vice president. He had thought he was in with the "powers that be," but he had found out the hard way that was wrong. Shortly after that, my former secretary got her walking papers as well. What hurt the most was the fact that she had lied about me in order to convince management that a change was necessary. I had taken good care of her and trusted her as well. She had pretended to be a God-fearing Christian woman. I know that all of this makes me sound bitter about these two individuals, but I'm not. I knew the truth, and I knew that eventually they were going to get what was coming to them. If you don't believe anything else I've said in this book, you had better believe me when I tell you "You reap what you sow," and "What goes around, comes around."

12

Why?

I'll give you a quick timeline so you can get your bearings here. I had major surgery in late January 2000. I was recovering at home on my birthday, which was on Thursday, February 10, and I got my billboard from God concerning my career choices the next day. On my way home from the meeting at the gas company, I called my dad and told him what was going on. He told me not to worry—God must want me to go into real estate full-time. One thing my dad would always bring up was that I should go to the high school and coach football. I always helped kickers and coaches if they asked me, but I wasn't the type to just go up to a school and say, "Here I am! I want to coach." A new high school was being built up the street from my house, and Dad thought it would be perfect for me. It was scheduled to open in August 2000, but they hadn't named a football coach yet.

I truly believe that God has plans for everyone's lives. This up-and-down roller coaster I was on was getting ready to jump the tracks. I spent that weekend working in real estate; after all, I had to get busy, since I was now self-employed. I told Dad that I had to get the ball rolling, so we made plans to sneak off on Tuesday and play golf. We played together at least once a week. I never really liked the sport, but he did. I was playing so we could hang out together. When I was a kid, he used to go off to play, but I couldn't go because I was still too young. I was thrilled to be able to hang out with him this way.

Tuesday came, but not in the way I had expected. My telephone rang at about six o'clock in the morning, and my mom was on the other end. She said that Delta had called, and they were taking my dad over to South Fulton Hospital. She wanted me to take her there so we could find out what was going on. In the car on our way there, we talked about how his blood pressure was probably high, and we guessed the nurse at Delta wanted it checked out. That had happened a few times before. My dad had high blood pressure and diabetes. When we arrived at the hospital, we were greeted by several Delta executives. I looked at Mom, and both of us were puzzled. All we were told was that the emergency room nurse wanted to know as soon as we got there.

The nurse took us back to the emergency room, where we were greeted by the specialist. Mom saw Dad lying there and went straight to him. I was left to talk to the doctor myself. He started to tell me that they had already figured out what was wrong with him. He had a cerebral hemorrhage, the doctor explained, and he went on to say he was sorry. I remember looking at him and saying, "Are you telling me my father is going to die?" He looked at me and said, "Yes." They had ruled out risking surgery, because cutting into his brain to find the leak was like looking for a needle in a haystack. The doctor said that the hemorrhage was very large and had caused my dad to have a stroke. "The fact is," he said, "you don't get any symptoms with this until it's too late. Most people don't live to make it to the hospital." I asked him if there was any hope at all. He said that if Dad made it through the next forty-eight hours, he might have a chance.

I went to my dad's bedside, where he was still awake and trying to talk. The stroke had caused his speech to slur, but I could still understand him. He looked at me and said, "The doctor tell you I had a stroke?" I just kept telling him to please rest, because it was very important that we get his blood pressure down. Mom began to ask me questions, and then simply said, "Well, it's not life-threatening. He's not going to die, is he?" I just looked at her and nodded my head yes.

I went out and told the Delta guys in the lobby what was going on. I told them that I had to get my brothers, sister, and uncle to the hospital quickly. My brother, Mark, was in Charlotte, and my Uncle John was in Massachusetts. Mr. Bohannon and Mr. Turner told me to call them and tell them to go straight to their respective airports. They were to identify themselves to Delta representatives when they get there, and the rest would be taken care of. My brother and uncle didn't get hassled about not having tickets; on the contrary, their planes was stopped at the end of the runway when it landed in Atlanta, they were taken off the back of the airplane, put in security cars, and rushed to South Fulton Hospital. I was raised a "Delta brat," and it was always viewed as the Delta family. Rumors at the time said it wasn't the same company anymore, it wasn't a family anymore. I'll never believe that, because the chips were down and Delta employees all around the country rallied to help one of their own in trouble. My family will always be in debt to Delta Air Lines and will always consider ourselves part of the family.

I was able to get all of the necessary family members to the hospital, and Dad was hanging on. The doctors were going to put him into a coma and try to stop the bleeding. Before he went under, he was still very coherent. He had a hard time speaking because of the stroke, but to be honest, he wouldn't shut up. The last words he spoke to me would be his last. "Don't let me die like Grandpa." I told him that I wouldn't.

His father had had a stroke and basically became a prisoner in his own body. Nana kept him alive on life support, and he had to have people do everything for him. Since my grandpa was so proud and strong, I think the helplessness was more torture for him than the stroke itself. I never knew my father to be afraid of anything or anyone, but he was afraid of dying like that.

They moved my dad to the intensive care unit, because, to the surprise of the doctors, he was still alive. The hospital began to get flooded with calls and people once the word got out that something was wrong with him. At one point, the director of the hospital came to me and asked me to ask people to stop calling. He said it was jamming the switchboard. I smiled with pride and said, "Sorry." After staying up around the clock for two days at my dad's bedside, we asked the doctors if they could do another CAT scan to see what was going on. They said that if he was still with us in the morning, they would do another one. Morning came, and we were feeling great. His blood pressure was stable, and he was still alive.

A nurse approached us and said that the doctor wanted to talk to us. She took us to a room, where the doctor was waiting. When I walked in, I was confident that we were going to get good news. I had prayed to God constantly for the past two days and begged him not to take my best friend. He was still with us, he had good blood pressure readings, and everything pointed to a possible miracle. I had been listening to a song on my headphones constantly. It was called "Shout to the Lord," and its lyrics were relevant. It became my constant prayer to God for help. One look at the doctor's face told me that our battle had suffered a miserable defeat.

"I'm sorry," he said. "The hemorrhage was three by six when your dad got here, and now it's up to four by eight. There is no brain activity. Technically, he's already gone." After the initial shock, I spoke up first. I explained to the doctor that we potentially had a problem. (This is one of the times when being the oldest in an Italian family really stinks.) I explained to the doctor, "My father did not have a living will or a 'Do Not Resuscitate' (DNR) order in writing. I have to tell you now that you are not allowed to put him on life support, and if you try, I will do whatever is necessary to keep it from happening. Those were my dad's last words to me in the emergency room, and I have to do what he says."

My mom was in agreement, so I turned to Uncle John. He said that he was with us, and that if we had made the decision to go the other way, he would have had to say something. The doctor told us that since my dad had expressed that wish to me, even though it wasn't in writing, it was still his wish. We left the room and told the rest of the family and friends the bad news. Uncle John and Aunt Chickie, Dad's only brother and sister, along with the rest of the family, would have to say their final goodbyes.

Me & Dad

It was early on Sunday morning when my dad took his last breath and left us. My mom and I were the only ones there at the time. We hadn't slept since arriving at the hospital on Tuesday. Standing next to my dad's body with my mom that morning, I felt it was the worst day of my life. I noticed that she was trying to get his wedding band off, but couldn't. My parents had been married for thirty-four years and had grown up together as kids. They had a pact that when one of them died, the other would take off the wedding ring and wear it. Since she couldn't get the ring off, and with tears in her eyes, she asked me to remove the ring. His hands were swollen, and I felt his finger break as I was removing the ring. The moment his ring passed the end of his finger, my entire body became numb, and it has remained somewhat like that ever since. I took Mom home and began to make the arrangements. I handled pretty much everything, even previewing his body at the funeral home before my mom was allowed to view it for the first time. My mom picked out what she wanted him to be buried in. It was a Patriots golf shirt. When I saw it, I didn't say anything. I just gave it to the funeral director. When it came to the Patriots, anything I had, he had an identical match and vise-versa. To this day, my matching shirt like the one he's buried in, hangs in my closet.

13

Because God Has a Plan

After everything was over with, I couldn't help but believe my dad had some kind of idea that he was going to die soon. I know that sounds crazy, but let me explain. He did too many uncharacteristic and strange things right before he died. When it was determined that I needed testing and would need emergency surgery, my dad took me to the hospital visits. When I came home from the hospital, mostly out of it, I would awaken in the living room of my home and he would be sitting there with me.

There was a picture of the two of us at my last football game in college. We were cutting up in the stands after the game, and he grabbed me by the face and kissed me on the cheek. Someone took a picture of it. What was strange was that I hadn't seen the picture in years, but he blew it up, signed it, and framed it on his own. All he wrote on the picture was: "Even dads can love. Love, Dad 2000." His actual date of death was February 20, 2000.

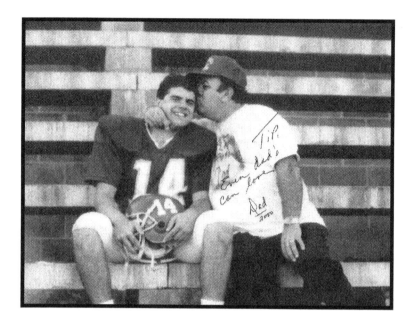

Another thing that was very strange was a phone call he made to Debbie late one night. It was a few weeks before he died, and I was sitting watching television. I knew that Debbie was on the phone, but I didn't pay much attention to it. Afterward, she came over and said to me, "That was strange." She told me that it was my dad on the phone. He had told her how much he loved her and how thankful he was to her for giving him his grandchildren. He also had told her what a great person she was and that he was so thankful she was a part of the family. After hearing this, my only reply was, "Call my mom. Something is wrong." Debbie replied, "No, it might embarrass him, and the call was for me. It was between him and me." I let it drop, as she had requested. It didn't come up again until Debbie mentioned it to my mom at the hospital. Mom had no idea he had called Debbie, and she was very surprised. After all, she knew him better than anyone, and she knew that was very strange.

I've heard stories of people getting a "heads up" that they needed to clear up unfinished business. I think it happened to my dad, and he didn't let on. I wish I had gotten the "heads up."

My dad was my best friend. There were times when I couldn't stand him or when he frustrated me to no end, but without a doubt, he was my hero. I made a videotape in college one year and put some highlights on it for him. The background music was "Wind Beneath My Wings," by Bette Midler. That became our song, because he was a big part of what made me tick. He would encourage, frustrate, and protect me in any way he could.

After his death, I grew angry with my spiritual father as well. Some of you will disagree with this part, but at least hear me out. I loved my father unconditionally. He was my hero who could do no wrong in my eyes. I wanted to be just like him. He also really ticked me off sometimes. That didn't mean there was ever a time I didn't love him. The one thing I'm grateful for is that he died with no regrets on my part. What I mean is that I didn't have to spend my last minutes with him telling him how much I loved him or that I was sorry for something. He knew that I loved him and I knew he loved me back. I looked at my relationship with God the same way. I was pretty angry at him for everything that had happened over the last few months, especially losing my dad. It's easy to say you have a good relationship with God when times are good, but how is it when the stuff hits the fan? My relationships with my spiritual father and my earthly father were a lot alike.

I also got sick of hearing about how God has a plan and how his will is always for good, never for bad. Everyone agrees with the concept of God's will. The bump in the road comes when our wills for our lives and God's will hit that fork in the road. You know what I mean here. Everything is great when the two wills are rocking along together on the same path, but the minute God's will for us goes in the opposite direction from what we want, that's when it gets touchy. I believe that all healthy relationships hit bumps in the road sooner or later. I hadn't stopped loving God; I was just ticked at him.

I still haven't yet dealt with my dad's death and probably won't ever deal with it. I look for him everywhere I go, and I swear I think I have seen him a couple of times since his death. Maybe it's wishful thinking, but I am intent on believing he's still with me every day. It's funny how when things are going bad and I'll get frustrated from time to time, I'll happen to turn on the radio and "Wind Beneath My Wings" will be playing. I think it's his way of saying "I still have your back, pal. Hang in there."

A few months after my dad's death, I happened to read in the paper the announcement for the new head coach at the high school. The new school up the street from my house was to be called Union Grove High School. The new head coach and athletic director was Scott Mason. Scott and I had been teammates in college together our whole career. You become close with your teammates while you're going through all the hardships of a football life. It's strange; you can go years without seeing a former teammate, but when you do, it's like you played with them yesterday. Once that bond is formed, it lasts forever. I was very happy that Scott was going to get his chance to run a program. My parents have always been fond of him. My dad would go to the other high school games, where Scott was an assistant coach, just to say hello to him and show support. I don't believe that it was a coincidence that Scott was named to the position right after my father passed. I'm sure dad had something to do with it from heaven.

I heard that the team was going to have a scrimmage against other county schools, so I decided to ride up there and wish Scott well with his new program. When he saw me before it started, he told me to stand with him on the sidelines during the scrimmage. Standing there, I could feel a burning in my gut. Boy, did I miss this. Afterward, Scott asked me if I could help coach the team that year. Even though I wasn't a certified teacher, the State of Georgia allows for people in the community to coach at the high school level. The only thing I would have to do was to take a couple of courses and pass the tests. All you need after that is to have a head coach, athletic director, and principal that wanted to hire you. I remember lying in my bed the night of the scrimmage saying out loud, "Okay, Dad—you win."

Now I had two full-time jobs: one as an entrepreneur in real estate, and another as a varsity football coach at Union Grove High School. The first football season for the school was pretty rough. We didn't win a game. Scott kept preaching to the kids that we were on a three-year plan, so stay positive. After all, we had freshman and sophomores playing a varsity schedule. The second year showed improvement; we surprised two teams and were able to pick up two victories that year. I know that it doesn't sound like much to get excited about, but some teams scored over seventy points against us that first year. One big change that we made for the second year was hiring Mike McDonald as our defensive coordinator. Mike and I came from the same high school in Morrow, but he was also a teammate of ours at Tennessee Wesleyan. We had three former teammates on the same coaching staff.

I started to develop a tight friendship with our kicker during the first season. I knew he was a special kid from the first time I met him. He was a good student and a good athlete and came from a great family. His name was Nick Ellis, and I began to teach him how to play all three kicking positions. He punted, kicked field goals, and kicked off for us. I never had anyone teach me the mechanics on kicking when I was his age. I didn't even find anyone who knew anything about it until I met Coach Roseberry during my senior year of college. Nick continued to improve, and I knew he had turned into a weapon that we would be able to use in our third year. His ultimate goal was to earn a college scholarship to play football, and I was determined to do everything in my power to help him get it.

There was a lot of pressure on the coaching staff to have a successful third year. After all, we had barked about a three-year plan. Guess what? Year Three was here. High schools in Henry County pretty much had the reputation of being pitiful when it came to any type of success in football. The season was going as planned, and Scott looked like a genius. We entered the last game of the season with a seven and two record. The last game against Grady High would be for the regional championship. The team had a great season going. All of the kids matured and grew together as a team. Nick hit field goals from forty-seven and forty-eight yards. His big one came against Decatur when he nailed a fifty-yard field goal to end the half. The place went crazy. It was the first time I had ever witnessed, in person, a high-school kicker hit from fifty yards in a game. He was punting very well and even had twenty-five touchbacks on kickoffs. You could tell that our kids were a little nervous against Grady High. We played the game like we were playing "not to lose," instead of "to win." When it was over, Union Grove became the first school in Henry County history to win a regional championship 17–14. The win also brought about another first for the county: Union Grove would host the first round of the state playoffs.

The atmosphere was electric for the first playoff game. The place was packed, and we were facing a very tough Lumpkin County team. The game was evenly matched, but eventually we took control and won. The win meant that we would also host the second round.

The second round brought Washington Wilkes High to town. Everyone in the papers (and stands, for that matter) picked Washington Wilkes to beat us by twenty-one points. To be honest, when they took the field to warm up, I thought to myself, *What a good-looking bunch of athletes.* We completed two touchdown passes early and took a 14–10 lead into the locker room at halftime. We preached to the kids about the importance of the first series of the second half. We were going to get the ball first and had to convert it into points.

We took the field for the second half and had our drive stall out around mid-field. It was fourth down and long. Conventional coaching says you punt the ball and pin them deep in their own territory. Sometimes you can't use conventional wisdom. I had been working on a fake punt all season, and felt we needed to use it now. We were twenty-one-point underdogs. If they got the ball back and scored, they would go up 17–14. No one would expect us to call a fake punt this early in the game, especially since it was the second round of the state playoffs. I convinced Scott, and he agreed for me to make the call. It was my turn to look like a genius, because the play I had affectionately named "The Militia Surprise" worked like a charm. Our kids executed it perfectly, and Eddie Gadson was finally tackled on Washington Wilkes' six-yard line. One play later, Joey Waters kept the ball on the quarterback sneak for the score. We went up 21–10 and never looked back. That critical point of the game took all the wind out of our opponent. Instead of them beating us by twenty-one points, we went on to upset them by twenty-one: the final score was 42–21.

We would have to travel on to the quarter finals to face the two-time defending state champion, Americus High School. The school rented motor coaches for us to make the trip. As the buses left the school, the middle school and elementary school students, faculty, and fans lined the streets to wave us off and wish us well. It was awesome to see the community support for our kids, who had defied the odds so far. However, our Cinderella season would come to an end.

Americus was much too powerful for us on their home field, and we couldn't stop them. We came home totally dejected. Our improbable run was over.

No one can ever take away what these kids did accomplish. They became the first team in county history to win a regional championship, host a state playoff game, reach the quarter finals, and post ten wins in a season. We finished 10–3. Our first senior class was a special group of kids. After going 2–20 in their first two seasons, they finished year three at 10–3: the fastest turnaround for a new school in the state. I don't worry about our kids who graduated that year. They are champions, and they will be champions in life as well. I was fortunate to be named "Assistant Coach of the Year" in *Kudzu Life Magazine.* Scott earned many head coaching honors for that season from multiple organizations. It couldn't have happened to a better friend.

Five of our kids from that team went on to play in college. Nick reached his goal and earned a Division One scholarship to play at Charleston Southern University. He became their starting kicker and punter in his freshman year. His fifty-yard field goal is still a record for the southern crescent, in addition to other kicking records he set. He worked hard, had a dream, and went and got it. He still comes home to train with me over the summer. He'll never know how proud I am of him.

I can't help but think that the emphasis our staff put on the Militia, played a big part in our team's overall success that third year. "The Militia" is the name I came up with for our special teams unit. I have a strong, aggressive philosophy when it comes to special teams play. Most teams simply look at special teams as something you do in between offense and defense. This is ironic, because about every game, in my opinion, is won or lost with special teams. Coach Mason and I agreed that we would try our best to turn the Militia into a weapon. We would try to beat our opponents on all three sides of the football.

I am confident in my knowledge of special teams and my ability to teach special teams play. The biggest obstacle to overcome is getting the kids to buy into the philosophy. Whether you are talking about sports or business, if your team doesn't totally believe in what you are doing, you will not be successful. All objectives requiring a team's involvement need the support and enthusiasm of the entire team to be successful. I was battling with the misconception that special teams play was reserved for the kids on the team that might not be good enough to earn a playing spot on offense or defense. I am committed to changing that type of mentality.

It was very important to have the coaching staff and the kids buy into what we were trying to do with the Militia. Once we announced that we would form the Militia, we had tryouts to see which kids on the team would make the squad. A player's initial selection to the Militia was based on these criteria: ability, attitude, desire, and overall commitment to the team and to the classroom. Players would be evaluated in spring practice and off-season workouts. I came up with a logo for the Militia and bought T-shirts that only the members could wear. The players knew that being a part of this unit was a privilege, not a right. They could be removed from the Militia if they did not perform or conduct themselves honorably. If someone had to be removed from the Militia, he would have to give back his T-shirt and helmet decal. If members still had the shirts after the last game, then and only then were they theirs to keep.

Over the years, the T-shirt has become a prized possession with the players. To be honest, it has almost gotten me in trouble a couple of times. Let me explain. The original logo was the Minute Man, which is recognized as a national monument. I had to come up with something else, because some people in the county office had a problem with it. Are you ready to hear what their problem was? The icon representing the Minute Man showed him holding an old rifle from the American Revolution. Higher-ups at the board of education had a problem with it, because they were trying so hard to keep guns out of the schools; since the symbol was holding one, they didn't like it. Give me a break. It's in every history book in the school, it's a national monument, and it's on the Massachusetts state quarter. Sometimes I think society and the "powers that be" overexaggerate things.

The other time the shirt almost got me in trouble was when someone other than a player wore it. The parents wanted to buy them, but they were not for sale, and parents were not allowed to wear them either. Wives count, too. My wife, who knew it was a big no-no for her to wear it, decided to wear it under a shirt to school one day. Of course, it was my shirt she wore, and she did it on a dare from one of the other coaches. Needless to say, when I found out, it wasn't a pretty sight. The players didn't like it either.

The Militia was based on the principles of strength and honor. We wanted to be known as mentally and physically strong. We also wanted the reputation of being honorable. I felt that this helps instill pride and values in the kids. The principles of the Militia were not only for the football field, but for the classroom and the community as well. I felt it necessary to hold these guys accountable, because life sure will. Every time we broke the Militia huddle, it was to the tune of "TTFP." This outlined the main objective and goal focus for the Militia on the field. "TTFP" stands for Touchdowns, Turnovers, and Field Position. If we could accomplish these three objectives, we would win the football game. The Militia had a different captain for each game that represented the unit at the coin toss. It has even evolved in the community: Chick-Fil-A sponsors a Minute Man player of the week and treats that player to a free dinner.

2004 UGHS Kickers

Special teams play and strategy is my passion on the football field. I like defense, I love offense, but my passion is special teams. Unfortunately, people only remember the things that go wrong when it comes to special teams. We have recovered surprise onsides kicks, executed fakes punts, run punts and kickoffs back for touchdowns, and pinned teams deep in their own zone. Give up a kickoff or two and that's all you hear about.

In 2003, we were playing Crim High out of Atlanta. We scored fourteen points at the beginning of the game, and Crim ran the ensuing kickoff back for a touchdown. What made it a nightmare was the fact that we scored again to go up 21–7, and they ran the next kickoff back for a touchdown. Their first fourteen points came on kickoff returns for touchdowns. To add to my frustration, when they kicked off to us, they kicked an onsides kick every time. That was a testament of respect for our kickoff return unit, who had scored against other teams and was averaging over thirty yards a return. Crim figured they would just give us the ball at midfield rather than giving up a touchdown. We managed to get up on Crim thirty-five to fourteen when things started to go sour. They threw some long passes for scores and intercepted one of our passes for a touchdown, tying the score at thirty-five. Momentum is a huge advantage in a football game, and it was all with them now. What happened next is a prime example of how special teams can turn a game.

Once they tied the score, they did the unthinkable: they kicked the ball deep to us. Eighty-five yards later, we were in the end zone to retake the lead and momentum, which put us in front for good. I couldn't believe that after they had onsides kicked to us the whole game, the only time they kicked deep, we returned it for a touchdown. The most frustrating thing about this game was the fact that we set a Militia record for points in a game. Our goal was to put up at least ten points in a game, and in this game against Crim, we scored nineteen. What stinks is that all anyone remembers is the first two touchdowns we gave up. The final score was fifty-five to forty-two. What we did on special teams in that game was unbelievable, but I'll hear about those first two touchdowns until the day they bury me.

Over the years, I had always helped young kickers and punters based on their individual requests, but I felt that I should try to branch out and help more kids. I never had a kicking coach, except for my dad, so I wanted to see if I could provide instruction and motivation on a wider scale. I decided to form a kicking school where kids could come for my help and get the one-on-one attention they would need in order to become successful. I formed The Kicking Machine in 2001, and it has become another blessing in my life. I know that it was what God wanted, because the kids he has sent to me have become a huge part of my extended family. How I have come to meet them is truly God's work.

I want to mention these kids because their stories really drive home the fact that God has a plan, and if you are open to it, you will be blessed in ways that you never imagined possible.

Doug Carter was the first kicker I developed a relationship with after meeting Nick. Doug had never played football before and wanted to come to the kicking school and learn. Kicking is the most difficult skill to master on the football field. I know it looks easy, but grab a football and try it—you'll see it's not easy. It takes a lot of dedication to do it well, and even then, you might not do it correctly all the time. Doug worked his tail off; he was dedicated to his goal of becoming a varsity kicker, and he did reach that dream. I tell the kids that where you start is not important, but where you finish is. Doug is proof of how perseverance and commitment can take you up to your dream. I am so proud of him and thankful for having him in my family.

I met another one of my students in a bizarre way. One year, I went to watch a state championship football game in south Georgia with Coach Mac. The stadium was packed, and we were literally packed in. After halftime, Joe talked me into moving to the other end of the field, so we could look for a better place to see the game. I didn't want to move, but if you know Coach Mac, well...he convinced me to move. We ended up sitting on the ground, peeking through a chain-link fence at the back of the end zone. That's where God introduced me to Sean.

Sean Mayo was the kid that just happened to sit down next to me on the ground, trying to peek through the same fence. Coach Mac and I were watching the halftime warm-ups, and I was talking to him about the kickers on the field. Sean struck up a conversation with me, saying that he happened to be a kicker. He asked if I would be willing to work with him, and I agreed. We left that night with the understanding that I would send him my contact information, and that if he still wanted to learn, he would let me know. I really didn't expect to hear back from him. See, he lives and plays at a high school that is at least an hour-and-a-half drive (one way) from where I live. At best, I expected him to make the trip once. I underestimated Sean's desire. For several months, he made that trip to practice with me at least twice a week, and sometimes he came up three times a week. He is a great kid, and he has become an important part of my life.

A great reward came for me when I received a phone call from him over Christmas break during his senior season. Sean had been selected to play in the North *vs.* South All-Star Classic, and he wanted to know if I would drive to Columbus for the game. He was the only kicker selected for the South Squad; what a huge honor. The fact that he wanted me to be there meant the world to me. I told him that I wouldn't miss it for anything. He went on to receive numerous post-season awards, including first team All-State. He deserves everything he gets in life, and there is no doubt that if he wants it, he'll go get it.

I don't know where yet, but I do know that Doug and Sean will be playing for colleges next year. The schools that get them will be getting two role models both on and off the field. What's great for me is that even though they will be moving away for college, I know they will stay in touch through the weeks and come home to train with me over the summer, the way Nick still does.

Some of my young players, like Macklin, Evan, and Stephen, are making great strides and learning how dreams are reachable. You just have to be dedicated and never stop believing it's possible.

These kids have become an important part of my family. They are great role models for my children, and the bottom line is that God put them there. I am thankful to God for putting them in my life, and I'm glad that I was open enough to accept this blessing. These kids don't know it, but they give me the strength to keep going every day, no matter how many times life kicks me in the teeth.

I can't wait to meet God's next blessing.

14

The Moral of the Story

What have I learned so far in my life? I've learned that there are good times and bad. Neither one can go on forever. You must try to enjoy the good times, and hold on through the bad times. I reference a lot of different quotes in this book, none of which I came up with myself, but I am thankful that there are smart people out there who did, because these quotes of inspiration have become my battle cry. You can't quit when the bad times are here. One saying that is at the top of my list is this one from the Bible: "Trust in the Lord with all your heart and lean not unto your own understanding, but in all your ways acknowledge him and he will direct your paths" (Prov. 3:5–6). Make that verse your foundation, and you will be able to deal with life's roller coaster ride. Just trust that God knows what he's doing and you don't, and you'll be okay.

I just completed my fifth season as the special teams (Militia) kickers and wide receivers coach, and finished my sixth year in real estate. I hold my own kicking camp over the summer, where high school and college kickers come to learn the mechanics that will hopefully get them closer to their goals. I have been asked to speak words of encouragement at several different functions that involve young people. I have been blessed by God in more ways than I can count. I am even up for induction into my college's Hall of Fame, and my picture's up at my old high school in Morrow. I don't think that's too bad for a kid with limited athletic ability but a whole lot of "want to." Only God knows what he has in store for the rest of my life. I'm just along for the ride, doing the best I can—the same way you are.

The moral of the story is simple. Trust in God and believe in yourself. Your worst enemy is you. Love people, and they will love you back. You can have whatever you desire if you want it badly enough and you are willing to pay the price to get it. So many lessons I learned on the football field turned out to be applicable to living in general. Sometimes you score touchdowns, and sometimes you give them up. Fumbles and interceptions happen in football and in life. You have to make your own opportunities and sometimes take risks. Tough times never last, but tough people do.

I sometimes think about what would have happened if I had just quit along the way. What if I had followed through on my thoughts that night leaving the Waffle House? I know I would have missed having the three most precious gifts God ever gave me: my three children. My kids know that their dad isn't perfect, but they also know he is a fighter. I realize that sometimes they might think that events in my life are more important to me than they are, but there is nothing further from the truth. Everything I do in my life is for them, and it means a lot to me to make them proud. As a father, it is very difficult to juggle everything at once. If I could, I would spend every minute of the day with them, but unfortunately, I can't. I just don't want them to ever feel that they are second to anything in my life, because they are not. I believe every father goes through these feelings of inadequacy from time to time. One thing is certain: I would give up my life for my children, and I want them to know that. This book is my way of letting them know that their daddy loves them with all his heart. I will always love them, no matter what. Nothing and no one could ever take their place, and I wouldn't have it any other way.

Anthony, Anissa & Antonia

I am also thankful for all my players at Union Grove High School. No matter where life takes us, we will always be family.

Will Always Be Home

Quitting is never an option for me, and it shouldn't be for you, either. I miss my dad every day, but each time I hit the football field on Friday night, I can't help but feel him standing next to me through every minute of the game. Those are really the hardest times, because I really miss being able to talk to him. I miss getting his advice and spending time with him.

Everything I do is done in an effort to make my family proud. My mom and dad will always be my heroes, along with my brothers and sister. Hopefully, one day this book will serve as inspiration to the loves in my life: my family. After all, they have been my inspiration.

You have to get out there and live life. There is nothing wrong with attempting something and failing. You learn your greatest lessons through failure. People will criticize you and your actions. If you do fail, then they will criticize that as well. Nothing in this world worth having comes easily. Success is nothing more than a series of failures multiplied by perseverance. I would rather try to make a difference, and fail, than not try at all. I think one of our country's greatest presidents said it best in the following quote:

> It is not the critic who counts; not the man who points out where the strong man stumbled or the doer of deeds could have done better. The credit belongs to the man who is actually in the arena whose faced is marred by the dust, the sweat, and the blood; who strives valiantly; who errs and comes up short again and again; who knows the great enthusiasms and the great devotions; who spends himself in a worthy cause; who in the end, at best, knows the triumph of high achievement, and at worst, if he fails, at least fails while daring greatly, so that his place shall never be among those cold and timid souls who know neither victory nor defeat.—Theodore Roosevelt

In football, a team is sometimes faced with the situation of "fourth down and long." Some teams get themselves in this situation more than others, and when faced with it, there are only two options. You can either gamble and call a fake punt, or you can punt the ball away and hope you can play good defense.

My life has been a series of "fourth down and longs," on the field and off it. I'm sure it has been for you as well. Football is like life, and life is a lot like football. Sometimes I choose to take a risk and execute a fake. You just have to take those risks from time to time and go against conventional wisdom. Other times, you can do what I do best. Just punt the ball away and live to fight another series.

Vinny, Scotty, Me, Mom, Dad, Gina, & Mark

2004 - My Family

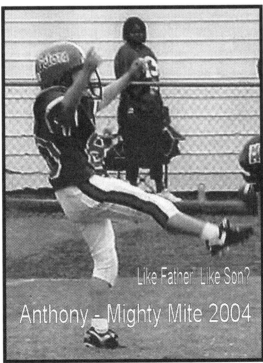

Like Father. Like Son?

Anthony - Mighty Mite 2004

One Final Thought

Well, here it is: my book. The purpose of this book is to give my children and family something to keep forever. I wrote it for a few reasons. First off, it has been on my list of life goals since I was a kid. I wanted to prove to myself that I could write a book, even though most people would have said I couldn't. It has taken me almost four years—off and on—to get to this final thought. I'm sure most authors could have done it in less time, but sorry, I'm not one of them. I just stayed true to the dream of writing it and…wrote it. I tell you this because if it is a dream for you, you can do it too. It's not easy, but it is possible.

The main reason I wrote this was for my children and family. I wanted them to have something that would last forever. I know my family will keep it, and share it with future family members as well. I want them to know that life will take you on a series of ups and downs, and you can make it through all of them. Just believe in God, and keep going. Don't ever give up on your dreams. I love you all very much.

I have been blessed with the opportunity to address young people at different functions, and will continue to do so when asked. I want them to know that sometimes in life, the underdog does win. Everybody is someone, and strangers are just friends you haven't met yet. Don't hurt someone else to get what you want out of life, because it's not necessary. There's an old saying that goes something like this: "Be careful of the toes you step on today, because they might be attached to the rear end you kiss tomorrow." Don't intentionally hurt anyone and you won't have to worry about it.

One thing that has helped me through the rough times is to force myself to read something positive and upbeat. I'm not a very good reader, but I have tried to force myself to read something positive and inspirational, even if it is just for a couple of minutes.

I would like to tell you a few of my favorites over the years and encourage you to read them as well. They are written by people more intelligent and educated than I am, but we do have at least one thing in common: we have all written a book. I want to share them with you here as my way of thanking these authors for taking the time and effort to put their thoughts on paper and helping me achieve my goals. These authors have no clue who I am, but maybe one day they'll know that they were inspirations in my life and helped me keep going when most people thought I should quit. They are as follows:

The Holy Bible. The greatest book ever written is full of inspiring quotes and answers to all life's questions. It will give you hope and comfort.

Winning 101 (Insight and Motivation to Help You Achieve Excellence), by Van Crouch (Honor Books). I refer to this book often, because it takes quotes and success stories and connects them to Bible verses. Whether you're an athlete or a business professional, you'll find several pages that you can refer to for help.

The Magic of Thinking Big, by David J. Schwartz, PhD (Simon & Schuster, Inc.). This book provides methods and motivation for believing in yourself and reaching for your dreams.

How to Win Friends & Influence People, by Dale Carnegie (Pocket Books). This book helps you to understand people and how to deal with them. This world is made up of all kinds of people, and it helps to get information on how to deal with them in your everyday life.

When God Doesn't Make Sense, by Dr. James Dobson (Tyndale House Publishers, Inc.). This book was given to me after my father passed away. It has been extremely helpful to me, and if you are dealing with the loss of a loved one, I strongly suggest you go and buy this book. It can't take the hurt away, but it can help explain the emotional struggles whenever you have to deal with heartache.

I hope my book has in some way touched your life. Hopefully, you can see that you, too can reach your dreams, as long as you fight for them and stay committed to them. Just remember that happiness is a state of mind, and life is what you make of it. For me, writing this book has been a long four-year struggle, but it was worth it. Now I can cross this goal off the sheet and move on down the list. Next up on the list will be a coaching job in college or the NFL. I'll put forth the effort; we'll just have to wait and see if my goal sheet still matches God's. After all, his goal sheet for me is the one that counts.

0-595-67095-4